D0795845

sweet and
savoury bites

Published in 2007 by Murdoch Books Pty Limited.
www.murdochbooks.com.au

Murdoch Books Australia
Pier 8/9, 23 Hickson Road
Millers Point NSW 2000
Phone: + 61 (0) 2 8220 2000
Fax: + 61 (0) 2 8220 2558

Murdoch Books UK Limited
Erico House, 6th Floor
93–99 Upper Richmond Road
Putney, London SW15 2TG
Phone: + 44 (0) 20 8785 5995
Fax: + 44 (0) 20 8785 5985

Chief Executive: Juliet Rogers
Publishing Director: Kay Scarlett

Concept & Art Direction: Sarah Odgers
Design: Jacqueline Duncan
Project Manager and Editor: Rhiain Hull
Production: Adele Troeger
Photographer: Jared Fowler
Stylist: Cherise Koch
Food preparation: Alan Wilson
Introduction text: Leanne Kitchen
Recipes developed by the Murdoch Books Test Kitchen

©Text, design and illustrations Murdoch Books Pty Limited 2007. All rights reserved. No part of this publication may be reproduced, stored in a retrieval system or transmitted in any form or by any means, electronic, mechanical, photocopying, recording or otherwise without the prior written permission of the publisher.

National Library of Australia Cataloguing-in-Publication Data
Sweet and savoury bites. Includes index.
ISBN 978 1 92125 906 7. ISBN 1 921259 06 X.
1. Appetizers. 2. Snack foods. I. Hull, Rhiain.
II. Price, Jane (Jane Paula Wynn). (Series: Kitchen classics; 5). 641.812

A catalogue record for this book is available from the British Library

Printed by 1010 Printing International Limited in 2007. PRINTED IN CHINA.
Reprinted 2007 (twice).

CONVERSION GUIDE: You may find cooking times vary depending on the oven you are using. For fan-forced ovens, as a general rule, set the oven temperature to 20°C (35°F) lower than indicated in the recipe. We have used 20 ml (4 teaspoon) tablespoon measures. If you are using a 15 ml (3 teaspoon) tablespoon, for most recipes the difference will not be noticeable. However, for recipes using baking powder, gelatine, bicarbonate of soda (baking soda) and small amounts of flour, add an extra teaspoon for each tablespoon specified.

sweet and savoury bites

THE SNACK-TIME RECIPES YOU MUST HAVE

SERIES EDITOR **JANE PRICE**

MURDOCH BOOKS

CONTENTS

HOME-MADE TREATS   6

SWEET BITES   8

SAVOURY BITES   92

TRADITIONAL BITES   136

KIDS' BITES   208

INDEX   250

HOME-MADE TREATS

In an arguably more civilised age, the world stopped for a mid-morning snack — and perhaps even for an afternoon one as well. Home baking was a regular activity, deliciously warm aromas permeated the kitchen and cake tins were filled for another week. Now, it seems, we're all far too busy to enjoy even a half-hour's pause over a cup of tea or freshly brewed coffee. Let alone devote time to baking 'from scratch'. Before we completely relinquish the joys of snack-time though, it's good to remind ourselves that, in an increasingly frantic world, it makes sense to pause from life's demands and take time for an energizing drink and a nibble of some delectable morsel.

This can be as intimate an affair as just you, a friend, a pot of coffee and a few slices of cake (be they banana, chocolate mud cake or strawberry swiss roll); or a plate of digestive biscuits served with glasses of milk to keep kids' after-school hunger pangs at bay. There are plenty of larger-scale occasions too, when loading a prettily-set table with muffins, scones, friands, tea cakes, cheesecakes, sausage rolls and the like, is perfectly appropriate. Bridal showers, birthday celebrations, anniversaries and pre-Christmas get-togethers are also excellent opportunities to buff up silver teapots, dust off fine, bone china and pass around plates of sweet and savoury goodies. And the fare, as this comprehensive collection of recipes demonstrates, can be as diverse and as flexible as you'd like — from heftier snack offerings like chicken tamales, roast capsicum rice tarts or generous slabs of lumberjack cake to more sophisticated nibbles such as crab and spring onion mini quiches, seafood parcels, duck tartlets and rich chocolate truffles. Rediscover the pleasures of the snack-time ritual with the deliciously timeless recipes here; they're as satisfying to make as they are to serve and to eat.

SWEET BITES

HAZELNUT AND CHOCOLATE FRIANDS

200 g (7 oz) hazelnuts

185 g (6^1/$_2$ oz) unsalted butter

6 egg whites

155 g (5^1/$_2$ oz/1^1/$_4$ cups) plain (all-purpose) flour

30 g (1 oz/^{1}/$_4$ cup) unsweetened cocoa powder

250 g (9 oz/2 cups) icing (confectioners') sugar

icing (confectioners') sugar, extra, to dust

MAKES 12

Preheat the oven to 200°C (400°F/Gas 6). Lightly grease a 12-hole friand tin.

Spread the hazelnuts out on a baking tray and bake for 8–10 minutes, or until fragrant (take care not to burn them). Wrap in a clean tea towel (dish towel) and rub vigorously to loosen the skins. Discard the skins. Cool, then process in a food processor until finely ground.

Melt the butter in a small saucepan over medium heat, then cook for 3–4 minutes, or until the butter turns deep golden. Strain to remove any residue (the colour will deepen on standing). Remove from the heat and set aside to cool to lukewarm.

Place the egg whites in a clean, dry bowl and lightly whisk until frothy but not firm. Sift the flour, cocoa powder and icing sugar into a large bowl and stir in the ground hazelnuts. Make a well in the centre, add the egg whites and butter and mix to combine.

Divide the mixture evenly among the friand holes — fill each hole to about three-quarters full. Place the tins on a baking tray and bake in the centre of the oven for 20–25 minutes, or until a skewer inserted into the centre of a friand comes out clean. Remove and leave to cool in the tins for 5 minutes before turning out onto a wire rack to cool completely. Dust with icing sugar before serving.

PREPARATION TIME: 20 MINUTES   COOKING TIME: 40 MINUTES

NOTE: These friands will keep for up to 4 days if stored in an airtight container.

SULTANA SCONES

250 g (9 oz/2 cups) self-raising flour
1 teaspoon baking powder
30 g (1 oz) unsalted butter, chilled and cubed
60 g (2¼ oz/½ cup) sultanas (golden raisins)
250 ml (9 fl oz/1 cup) milk
milk, extra, to glaze

MAKES 12

Preheat the oven to 220°C (425°F/Gas 7). Lightly grease a baking tray or line with baking paper. Sift the flour, baking powder and a pinch of salt into a bowl. Using your fingertips, rub in the butter until it resembles fine breadcrumbs. Stir in the sultanas. Make a well in the centre.

Add almost all the milk and mix with a flat-bladed knife, using a cutting action, until the dough comes together in clumps. Use the remaining milk if necessary. With floured hands, gently gather the dough together, lift out onto a lightly floured surface and pat into a smooth ball. Do not knead or the scones will be tough.

Pat the dough out to 2 cm (¾ inch) thick. Using a floured 5 cm (2 inch) cutter, cut into rounds. Gather the trimmings and without over-handling, press out as before and cut more rounds. Place close together on the tray and brush with the extra milk. Bake for 12–15 minutes, or until risen and golden brown. Serve warm or at room temperature.

PREPARATION TIME: 10 MINUTES   COOKING TIME: 15 MINUTES

PUMPKIN SCONES

250 g (9 oz) butternut pumpkin (squash), cut into cubes
250 g (9 oz/2 cups) self-raising flour
1 teaspoon baking powder
pinch freshly grated nutmeg
30 g (1 oz) unsalted butter, chilled and cubed
2 tablespoons soft brown sugar
125 ml (4 fl oz/½ cup) milk
milk, extra, to glaze

MAKES 12

Steam the pumpkin for 12 minutes, or until soft, then drain well and mash until smooth. Cool to room temperature. Preheat the oven to 220°C (425°F/Gas 7). Lightly grease a baking tray or line with baking paper.

Sift the flour, baking powder and a pinch of salt into a bowl and add the nutmeg. Using your fingertips, rub the butter into the flour, then stir in the sugar and make a well in the centre. Mix the milk into the pumpkin, add to the well in the flour and mix with a flat-bladed knife, using a cutting action, until the dough comes together in clumps. With floured hands, gather the dough together (it will be very soft) and lift out onto a lightly floured surface. Do not knead or the scones will be tough.

Pat the dough out to 2 cm (¾ inch) thick. Using a floured 5 cm (2 inch) cutter, cut into rounds. Gather the trimmings and, without over-handling, press out as before and cut out more rounds. Place the scones close together on the tray and brush with the extra milk. Bake for 12–15 minutes, or until risen and golden brown. Serve warm or at room temperature.

PREPARATION TIME: 15 MINUTES +   COOKING TIME: 30 MINUTES

Sultana scones

ORANGE POPPY SEED MUFFINS

310 g (11 oz/2$\frac{1}{2}$ cups) self-raising flour
40 g (1$\frac{1}{2}$ oz/$\frac{1}{4}$ cup) poppy seeds
80 g (2$\frac{3}{4}$ oz/$\frac{1}{3}$ cup) caster (superfine) sugar
125 g (4$\frac{1}{2}$ oz) unsalted butter
315 g (11$\frac{1}{4}$ oz/1 cup) orange marmalade
250 ml (9 fl oz/1 cup) milk
2 eggs
1 tablespoon finely grated orange zest

MAKES 12

Preheat the oven to 200°C (400°F/Gas 6). Lightly grease a 12-hole standard muffin tin, or line the muffin tin with paper cases. Sift the flour into a bowl. Stir in the poppy seeds and sugar, and make a well in the centre. Put the butter and 210 g (7$\frac{1}{2}$ oz/$\frac{2}{3}$ cup) of the marmalade in a small saucepan and stir over low heat until the butter has melted and the ingredients are combined. Cool slightly.

Whisk together the milk, eggs and orange zest and pour into the well. Add the butter and marmalade. Fold gently with a metal spoon until just combined. Do not overmix — the batter will still be slightly lumpy.

Divide the mixture evenly among the holes — fill each hole to about three-quarters full. Bake for 20–25 minutes, or until golden and a skewer inserted into the centre of a muffin comes out clean.

Heat the remaining marmalade and push it through a fine sieve. Brush generously over the top of the warm muffins. Leave them to cool in the tin for a couple of minutes. Gently loosen each muffin with a flat-bladed knife before turning out onto a wire rack. Serve warm or at room temperature.

PREPARATION TIME: 15 MINUTES   COOKING TIME: 30 MINUTES

NOTES: A variation of this muffin can be made using lime marmalade and finely grated lemon zest.

Muffins are most delicious if eaten on the day they are made and served warm. If you want to store muffins for a couple of days, let them cool completely, then store them in an airtight container. Muffins are also suitable for freezing.

BLUEBERRY MUFFINS

310 g (11 oz/2¹/₂ cups) self-raising flour
300 g (10¹/₂ oz) fresh blueberries
115 g (4 oz/¹/₂ cup) caster (superfine) sugar
375 ml (13 fl oz/1¹/₂ cups) milk
2 eggs, lightly beaten
1 teaspoon natural vanilla extract
150 g (5¹/₂ oz) unsalted butter, melted

MAKES 12

Preheat the oven to 200°C (400°F/Gas 6). Lightly grease a 12-hole standard muffin tin, or line the muffin tin with paper cases. Sift the flour into a bowl. Add the blueberries and sugar to the bowl and stir through the flour. Make a well in the centre. Mix together the milk, egg and vanilla. Pour the liquid into the well in the flour and add the butter. Fold the mixture gently with a metal spoon until just combined. Do not overmix — the batter will still be slightly lumpy. Divide the mixture evenly among the holes — fill each hole to about three-quarters full.

Bake the muffins for 20-25 minutes, or until golden and a skewer inserted into the centre of a muffin comes out clean. Leave them in the tin to cool for a couple of minutes. Gently loosen each muffin with a flat-bladed knife before turning out onto a wire rack. Serve warm or at room temperature.

PREPARATION TIME: 20 MINUTES   COOKING TIME: 25 MINUTES

NOTE: If fresh blueberries are unavailable, frozen ones can be used. Add while still frozen to avoid streaking the batter.

PECAN MUFFINS

310 g (11 oz/2¹/₂ cups) self-raising flour
90 g (3¹/₄ oz/³/₄ cup) chopped pecans
140 g (5 oz/³/₄ cup) soft brown sugar
375 ml (13 fl oz/1¹/₂ cups) milk
2 eggs, lightly beaten
1 teaspoon natural vanilla extract
150 g (5¹/₂ oz) unsalted butter, melted and cooled

MAKES 12

Preheat the oven to 200°C (400°F/Gas 6). Lightly grease a 12-hole standard muffin tin, or line the muffin tin with paper cases. Sift the flour into a bowl. Add the pecans and sugar to the bowl and stir through the flour. Make a well in the centre. Mix together the milk, egg and vanilla. Pour the liquid into the well in the flour and add the butter. Fold the mixture gently with a metal spoon until just combined. Do not overmix — the batter will still be slightly lumpy. Divide the mixture evenly among the holes — fill each hole to about three-quarters full.

Bake the muffins for 20-25 minutes, or until golden and a skewer inserted into the centre of a muffin comes out clean. Leave them in the tin to cool for a couple of minutes. Gently loosen each muffin with a flat-bladed knife before turning out onto a wire rack. Serve warm or at room temperature.

PREPARATION TIME: 20 MINUTES   COOKING TIME: 25 MINUTES

Blueberry muffins

ISRAELI DOUGHNUTS

185 ml (6 fl oz/³/₄ cup) lukewarm milk
1 tablespoon dried yeast
2 tablespoons caster (superfine) sugar
310 g (11 oz/2¹/₂ cups) plain (all-purpose) flour
2 teaspoons ground cinnamon
1 teaspoon finely grated lemon zest
2 eggs, separated
40 g (1¹/₂ oz) unsalted butter, softened
105 g (3³/₄ oz/¹/₃ cup) plum, strawberry or apricot jam
oil, for deep-frying
caster (superfine) sugar, extra, for rolling

MAKES 14

Put the milk in a small bowl, add the yeast and 1 tablespoon of the sugar. Leave in a warm, draught-free place for 10 minutes, or until bubbles appear on the surface. The mixture should be frothy and slightly increased in volume. If your yeast doesn't foam, it is dead, so you will have to discard it and start again.

Sift the flour into a large bowl and add the cinnamon, lemon zest, egg yolks, yeast mixture, remaining sugar, and a pinch of salt. Mix well, then place the dough on a lightly floured work surface and knead for 5 minutes. Work in the butter, a little at a time, continually kneading until the dough becomes elastic. This should take about 10 minutes. Place in a large bowl and cover with a clean, damp tea towel (dish towel). Leave to rise overnight in the refrigerator.

Place the dough on a lightly floured work surface and roll out to 3 mm (¹/₈ inch) thick. Using a 6 cm (2¹/₂ inch) cutter, cut 28 rounds from the dough. Place 14 of the rounds on a lightly floured tray and carefully place ³/₄ teaspoon of the jam into the centre of each. Lightly beat the egg whites, then brush a little around the outside edges of the rounds, being careful not to touch the jam at all. Top with the remaining 14 rounds and press down firmly around the edges to seal. Cover with a clean tea towel and leave to rise for 30 minutes. Make sure the dough has not separated at the edges. Press any open edges firmly together.

Fill a deep-fryer or large heavy-based saucepan one-third full of oil and heat to 170°C (325°F), or until a cube of bread dropped into the oil browns in 20 seconds. Cook the doughnuts in batches for 1¹/₂ minutes on both sides, or until golden. Drain on crumpled paper towels and roll in the extra caster sugar. Serve immediately.

PREPARATION TIME: 40 MINUTES +   COOKING TIME: 25 MINUTES

SPICY FRUIT BISCUITS

180 g (6½ oz) unsalted butter, softened
185 g (6½ oz/1 cup) soft brown sugar
1 teaspoon natural vanilla extract
1 egg
280 g (10 oz/2¼ cups) plain (all-purpose) flour
1 teaspoon baking powder
1 teaspoon ground mixed (pumpkin pie) spice
½ teaspoon ground ginger
95 g (3¼ oz/½ cup) fruit mince (mincemeat)

MAKES ABOUT 60

Cream the butter and sugar in a small bowl using electric beaters until light and fluffy. Add the vanilla and egg and beat until well combined. Transfer to a large bowl and add the sifted flour, baking powder, mixed spice and ground ginger. Using a flat-bladed knife, mix to a soft dough. Gather together, then divide the mixture into two portions. Roll one portion out on a sheet of baking paper to a rectangle about 2 mm (¹⁄₁₆ inch) thick and trim the edges. Repeat with the other portion of dough. Refrigerate until just firm.

Spread both portions of dough with the fruit mince and then carefully roll up Swiss-roll-style (jelly-roll-style). Refrigerate for 30 minutes, or until firm.

Preheat the oven to 180°C (350°F/Gas 4). Line two baking trays with baking paper. Cut the logs into slices about 1 cm (½ inch) thick. Place on the prepared trays, leaving 3 cm (1¼ inches) between each slice. Bake for 10–15 minutes, or until golden. Cool on the trays for 3 minutes before transferring to a wire rack to cool completely. When cold, store in an airtight container.

PREPARATION TIME: 30 MINUTES +   COOKING TIME: 15 MINUTES

GREEK SHORTBREAD

200 g (7 oz) unsalted butter, softened
125 g (4½ oz/1 cup) icing (confectioners') sugar, sifted
1 teaspoon finely grated orange zest
1 egg
1 egg yolk
310 g (11 oz/2½ cups) plain (all-purpose) flour
1½ teaspoons baking powder
1 teaspoon ground cinnamon
250 g (9 oz) blanched almonds, toasted, finely chopped
125 g (4½ oz/1 cup) icing (confectioners') sugar, extra, to dust

MAKES 38

Preheat the oven to 160°C (315°F/Gas 2–3). Line two baking trays with baking paper. Cream the butter, icing sugar and orange zest in a small bowl using electric beaters until light and fluffy. Add the egg and egg yolk and beat until thoroughly combined. Transfer the mixture to a large bowl.

Using a metal spoon, fold in the sifted flour, baking powder, cinnamon and almonds and mix until well combined.

Shape level tablespoons of mixture into crescent shapes and place on the trays. Bake for 15 minutes, or until lightly golden. Cool on the trays for 5 minutes before transferring to wire racks to cool completely. While still warm, dust heavily with half of the extra icing sugar. Just before serving, dust heavily again with the remaining icing sugar.

PREPARATION TIME: 40 MINUTES   COOKING TIME: 15 MINUTES

PECAN COFFEE SLICE

125 g (4$\frac{1}{2}$ oz/1$\frac{1}{4}$ cups) pecans
175 g (6 oz) blanched almonds
2 tablespoons plain (all-purpose) flour
165 g (5$\frac{3}{4}$ oz/$\frac{3}{4}$ cup) sugar
7 egg whites
dark unsweetened cocoa powder, to dust

COFFEE CREAM
200 g (7 oz) unsalted butter, cubed and softened
150 g (5$\frac{1}{2}$ oz) dark chocolate, melted and cooled
3-4 teaspoons instant coffee powder

MAKES 20

Preheat the oven to 180°C (350°F/Gas 4). Lightly grease a shallow 23 cm (9 inch) square tin and line with baking paper, leaving the paper hanging over on two opposite sides.

Roast the pecans and almonds on a baking tray for 5-10 minutes, or until golden. Cool slightly, then chop in a food processor until finely ground. Transfer to a bowl, add the flour and 110 g (3$\frac{3}{4}$ oz/$\frac{1}{2}$ cup) of the sugar and mix well. Beat the egg whites in a large dry bowl until soft peaks form. Gradually add the remaining sugar, beating until the mixture is thick and glossy and the sugar has dissolved. Gradually fold the nut mixture into the egg mixture, a third at a time, using a metal spoon. Spoon into the tin and smooth the surface. Bake for 20 minutes, or until springy when touched. Leave in the tin for 5 minutes, then lift out, using the paper as handles, and transfer to a wire rack to cool completely.

To make the coffee cream, beat the butter in a small bowl using electric beaters until light and creamy. Gradually pour in the cooled melted chocolate and beat well. Mix the coffee powder with 2 teaspoons water until dissolved, then add to the chocolate and mix well. Refrigerate for 5-10 minutes to thicken slightly.

Cut the slice in half horizontally with a sharp, serrated knife. Carefully remove the top layer and spread half the coffee cream over the base. Replace the top and spread evenly with the remaining cream. Run a palette knife backwards and forwards across the top to create a lined pattern, or use an icing (frosting) comb to create swirls. Refrigerate until firm. Trim the edges and cut into squares or fingers. Serve at room temperature or cold, dusted with dark cocoa powder or decorated with chocolate-coated or plain coffee beans, if desired. The slice can be refrigerated for up to 5 days.

PREPARATION TIME: 30 MINUTES +   COOKING TIME: 30 MINUTES

PLUM AND ALMOND SLICE

165 g (5³/4 oz) unsalted butter, cubed and softened

145 g (5¹/2 oz/²/3 cup) caster (superfine) sugar

2 eggs

60 g (2¹/4 oz/¹/2 cup) plain (all-purpose) flour

40 g (1¹/2 oz/¹/3 cup) cornflour (cornstarch)

2 tablespoons rice flour

1¹/2 tablespoons thinly sliced glacé ginger

825 g (1 lb 13 oz) tinned plums in syrup, drained, seeded and halved

90 g (3¹/4 oz/1 cup) flaked almonds

1 tablespoon honey, warmed

MAKES 9

Preheat the oven to 180°C (350°F/Gas 4). Lightly grease a 20 cm (8 inch) square tin and line with baking paper, leaving the paper hanging over the top edge of the tin on all sides. Cream the butter and sugar in a small bowl using electric beaters until light and fluffy. Add the eggs one at a time, beating well after each addition. Sift the flours over the mixture and fold into the mixture with the ginger. Spread into the tin. Arrange the plum halves on top, pressing them in. Scatter with the flaked almonds, pressing in gently, then drizzle with the honey.

Bake for 1 hour 10 minutes, or until firm and golden. Cover with foil if the slice starts to brown too much. Cool in the tin, then lift out, using the paper as handles, before cutting into pieces. The slice can be kept for up to 4 or 5 days if stored in an airtight container in the refrigerator.

PREPARATION TIME: 30 MINUTES   COOKING TIME: 1 HOUR 10 MINUTES

MACADAMIA BISCUITS

180 g (6¹/2 oz) unsalted butter, softened

185 g (6¹/2 oz/1 cup) soft brown sugar

1 teaspoon natural vanilla extract

1 egg

280 g (10 oz/2¹/4 cups) plain (all-purpose) flour

1 teaspoon baking powder

45 g (1³/4 oz/¹/2 cup) desiccated coconut

70 g (2¹/2 oz/¹/2 cup) chopped macadamia nuts, toasted

MAKES ABOUT 60

Cream the butter and sugar in a small bowl using electric beaters until light and fluffy. Add the vanilla and egg and beat until well combined. Transfer to a large bowl and add the sifted flour and baking powder, the coconut and the macadamia nuts. Using a flat-bladed knife, mix to a soft dough. Gather together, then divide the mixture into two portions.

Place one portion of the dough on a sheet of baking paper and press lightly until the dough is 30 cm (12 inches) long and 4 cm (1¹/2 inches) thick. Fold the paper around the dough and roll neatly into a log shape. Twist the edges of the paper to seal. Using a ruler as a guide, shape the logs into a triangle shape. Repeat the process with the other portion of dough. Refrigerate for 30 minutes, or until firm.

Preheat the oven to 180°C (350°F/Gas 4). Line two baking trays with baking paper. Cut the logs into slices about 1 cm (¹/2 inch) thick. Place on the prepared trays, leaving 3 cm (1¹/4 inches) between each slice. Bake for 10–15 minutes, or until golden. Cool on the trays for 3 minutes before transferring to a wire rack to cool completely. When cold, store in an airtight container.

PREPARATION TIME: 30 MINUTES +   COOKING TIME: 15 MINUTES

Plum and almond slice

CONTINENTAL SLICE

125 g (4$\frac{1}{2}$ oz) unsalted butter
115 g (4 oz/$\frac{1}{2}$ cup) caster (superfine) sugar
30 g (1 oz/$\frac{1}{4}$ cup) unsweetened cocoa powder
250 g (9 oz) shredded wheat biscuits, crushed
65 g (2$\frac{1}{2}$ oz/$\frac{3}{4}$ cup) desiccated coconut
30 g (1 oz/$\frac{1}{4}$ cup) chopped hazelnuts
60 g (2$\frac{1}{4}$ oz/$\frac{1}{4}$ cup) chopped glacé cherries
1 egg, lightly beaten
1 teaspoon natural vanilla extract

TOPPING
215 g (7$\frac{3}{4}$ oz/1$\frac{3}{4}$ cups) icing (confectioners') sugar
2 tablespoons custard powder or instant vanilla pudding mix
1 tablespoon Grand Marnier
60 g (2$\frac{1}{4}$ oz) unsalted butter
125 g (4$\frac{1}{2}$ oz) dark chocolate
60 g (2$\frac{1}{4}$ oz) Copha (white vegetable shortening)

MAKES 36

Line the base and sides of an 18 x 28 cm (7 x 11$\frac{1}{4}$ inch) shallow tin with foil. Combine the butter, sugar and cocoa powder in a small saucepan. Stir over low heat until the butter melts and the mixture is well combined. Cook, stirring, for 1 minute. Remove from the heat and cool slightly.

Combine the biscuit crumbs, coconut, hazelnuts and cherries in a large bowl. Make a well in the centre, then add the butter mixture, egg and vanilla all at once and stir well. Press the mixture firmly with the back of a spoon into the prepared tin. Refrigerate until firm.

To make the topping, combine the icing sugar with the custard powder. Mix the Grand Marnier with 1 tablespoon hot water. Beat the butter, using electric beaters, until creamy. Gradually add the sugar mixture and the Grand Marnier mixture, alternately, to the butter. Beat the mixture until light and creamy. Spread evenly over the base and then refrigerate until set.

Combine the chocolate and Copha in a heatproof bowl. Place the bowl over a saucepan of simmering water, making sure the base of the bowl does not touch the water, and stir over low heat until the chocolate melts and the mixture is smooth. Spread over the slice. Refrigerate for 4 hours or until firm. Cut the slice into squares to serve.

PREPARATION TIME: 30 MINUTES +   COOKING TIME: 5 MINUTES

27

LEMON AND LIME BISCUITS

150 g (5½ oz) unsalted butter, softened

170 g (6 oz/¾ cup) caster (superfine) sugar

1 egg, lightly beaten

1 tablespoon lime juice

2 teaspoons grated lime zest

2 teaspoons grated lemon zest

125 g (4½ oz/1 cup) plain (all-purpose) flour

60 g (2¼ oz/½ cup) self-raising flour

60 g (2¼ oz) marzipan, grated

LIME ICING

125 g (4½ oz/1 cup) icing (confectioners') sugar, sifted

1 teaspoon finely grated lime zest

1 tablespoon lime juice

MAKES 30

Line two baking trays with baking paper. Beat the butter and sugar in a bowl using electric beaters until light and creamy. Add the egg, lime juice, lime zest and lemon zest, beating until well combined.

Transfer the mixture to a large bowl. Using a flat-bladed knife, mix in the flours and marzipan to a soft dough. Divide the mixture in two. Turn one portion out onto a lightly floured surface and press together until smooth.

Form the biscuit dough into a log shape about 4 cm (1½ inches) in diameter. Wrap the log in plastic wrap and refrigerate for 1 hour. Repeat the process with the remaining dough. Preheat the oven to 180°C (350°F/Gas 4). Cut the dough into 1 cm (½ inch) slices. Place the slices on the prepared trays and bake for 10–15 minutes, or until the biscuits are lightly golden. Leave on the trays until cool.

To make the icing (frosting), place the icing sugar, lime zest and juice and 2 teaspoons water in a small bowl. Stir to combine. Beat the mixture until smooth. If the mixture is too thick, add a little extra juice or water. Dip the cooled biscuits in the icing. Decorate, if desired.

PREPARATION TIME: 40 MINUTES + COOKING TIME: 10–15 MINUTES

CHOCOLATE BROWNIES

40 g (1½ oz/⅓ cup) plain (all-purpose) flour

60 g (2¼ oz/½ cup) unsweetened cocoa powder

440 g (15½ oz/2 cups) sugar

120 g (4¼ oz/1 cup) chopped pecans or walnuts

250 g (9 oz) good-quality dark chocolate, chopped into small pieces

250 g (9 oz) unsalted butter, melted

2 teaspoons natural vanilla extract

4 eggs, lightly beaten

MAKES 24

Preheat the oven to 180°C (350°F/Gas 4). Lightly grease a 20 x 30 cm (8 x 12 inch) cake tin and line with baking paper, leaving the paper hanging over on the two long sides.

Sift the flour and cocoa powder into a bowl and add the sugar, nuts and chocolate. Mix together and make a well in the centre.

Pour the butter into the dry ingredients with the vanilla and eggs and mix well. Pour into the tin, smooth the surface and bake for 50 minutes (the mixture will still be a bit soft on the inside). Chill for at least 2 hours before lifting out, using the paper as handles, and cutting into pieces.

PREPARATION TIME: 20 MINUTES + COOKING TIME: 50 MINUTES

MAPLE AND PECAN BISCUITS

185 g (6¹/₂ oz) unsalted butter, softened
185 g (6¹/₂ oz/1 cup) soft brown sugar
60 ml (2 fl oz/¹/₄ cup) maple syrup
1 teaspoon natural vanilla extract
1 egg
280 g (10 oz/2¹/₄ cups) plain (all-purpose) flour
1 teaspoon baking powder
120 g (4¹/₄ oz/1 cup) finely chopped pecans
pecans, to decorate

MAKES ABOUT 60

Cream the butter and sugar in a small bowl using electric beaters until light and fluffy. Add the maple syrup, vanilla and egg and beat until well combined. Transfer to a large bowl and add the sifted flour and baking powder. Using a flat-bladed knife, mix to a soft dough. Gather together, then divide the mixture into two portions.

Place one portion of the dough on a sheet of baking paper and press lightly until the dough is 30 cm (12 inches) long and 4 cm (1¹/₂ inches) thick. Roll neatly into a log shape, then roll the log in the chopped pecans. Repeat the process with the other portion of dough and refrigerate for 30 minutes, or until firm.

Preheat the oven to 180°C (350°F/Gas 4). Line two baking trays with baking paper. Cut the logs into slices about 1 cm (¹/₂ inch) thick. Press a whole pecan into the top of each biscuit. Place on the prepared trays, leaving 3 cm (1¹/₄ inches) between each slice. Bake for 10–15 minutes, or until golden. Cool on the trays for 3 minutes before transferring to a wire rack to cool completely. When cold, store in an airtight container.

PREPARATION TIME: 30 MINUTES +   COOKING TIME: 15 MINUTES

CRUNCHY PEANUT MERINGUE SLICE

125 g (4¹/2 oz/1 cup) plain (all-purpose) flour
2 teaspoons icing (confectioners') sugar
80 g (2³/4 oz) unsalted butter, cubed
1 tablespoon iced water
105 g (3³/4 oz/¹/3 cup) apricot jam

NUT MERINGUE
240 g (8³/4 oz/1¹/2 cups) peanuts, roughly chopped
170 g (6 oz/³/4 cup) caster (superfine) sugar
30 g (1 oz/¹/3 cup) desiccated coconut
1 egg white

MAKES 20

Preheat the oven to 180°C (350°F/Gas 4). Lightly grease a shallow tin measuring 18 x 28 cm (7 x 11¹/4 inches) and line with baking paper, leaving the paper hanging over on the two long sides.

Put the flour, icing sugar and butter in a food processor and mix in short bursts until fine and crumbly. Add the iced water and process until the mixture just comes together. Turn the dough out onto a floured surface, gather into a smooth ball, then press out evenly, using floured hands or the base of a floured glass, to cover the base of the tin. Prick well and bake for 15 minutes, or until golden. Cool for 10 minutes before spreading the jam evenly over the surface.

To make the meringue, put all the ingredients in a large saucepan and stir with a wooden spoon over low heat until just lukewarm. Spread over the slice and bake for 20 minutes, or until the topping is golden and crisp. When cool, lift out, using the paper as handles, and cut into pieces.

PREPARATION TIME: 20 MINUTES +   COOKING TIME: 40 MINUTES

ANISEED BISCUITS

375 g (13 oz/3 cups) plain (all-purpose) flour
125 ml (4 fl oz/¹/2 cup) olive oil
125 ml (4 fl oz/¹/2 cup) beer
60 ml (2 fl oz/¹/4 cup) anisette liqueur
115 g (4 oz/¹/2 cup) caster (superfine) sugar
40 g (1¹/2 oz/¹/4 cup) sesame seeds
2 tablespoons aniseeds

MAKES 16

Preheat the oven to 200°C (400°F/Gas 6). Lightly grease a baking tray and line with baking paper. Sift the flour and 1 teaspoon salt into a large bowl and make a well in the centre. Add the oil, beer and anisette and mix with a large metal spoon until the dough comes together. Transfer to a lightly floured surface and knead for 3–4 minutes, or until smooth. Divide the dough into two, then divide each portion into eight. In a small bowl, combine the sugar, sesame seeds and aniseeds.

Make a small pile of the seed mix on a work surface and roll out each portion of dough over the mix to a 15 cm (6 inch) round with the seeds embedded underneath. Place the rounds on a baking tray with the seeds on top and bake for 5–6 minutes, or until the bases are crisp. Place 10 cm (4 inches) below a grill (broiler) for about 40 seconds, or until the sugar caramelizes and the surface is golden. Transfer to a wire rack to cool.

PREPARATION TIME: 15 MINUTES   COOKING TIME: 35 MINUTES

Crunchy peanut meringue slice

VIENNESE FINGERS

100 g (3½ oz) unsalted butter, softened
40 g (1½ oz/⅓ cup) icing (confectioners') sugar
2 egg yolks
1½ teaspoons natural vanilla extract
125 g (4½ oz/1 cup) plain (all-purpose) flour
100 g (3½ oz) dark chocolate, chopped
30 g (1 oz) unsalted butter, extra

MAKES 20

Preheat the oven to 180°C (350°F/Gas 4). Line two baking trays with baking paper.

Cream the butter and icing sugar in a small bowl using electric beaters until light and fluffy. Gradually add the egg yolks and vanilla and beat thoroughly. Transfer to a large bowl, then sift in the flour. Using a knife, mix until the ingredients are just combined and the mixture is smooth.

Spoon the mixture into a piping (icing) bag fitted with a fluted 1 cm (½ inch) piping nozzle and pipe the mixture into wavy 6 cm (2½ inch) lengths on the trays. Bake for 12 minutes, or until golden brown. Cool slightly on the trays before transferring to a wire rack to cool completely.

Place the chocolate and extra butter in a small heatproof bowl. Half-fill a saucepan with water and bring to the boil, then remove from the heat. Sit the bowl over the pan, making sure the base of the bowl does not touch the water. Stir occasionally until the chocolate and butter have melted and the mixture is smooth. Dip half of each biscuit into the melted chocolate mixture and leave to set on baking paper or foil. Store in an airtight container for up to 2 days.

PREPARATION TIME: 20 MINUTES +   COOKING TIME: 12 MINUTES

NOTE: To make piping easier, fold down the bag by about 5 cm (2 inches) before spooning the mixture in, then unfold. The top will be clean and easy to twist, thereby stopping the mixture from squirting out the top.

MONTE CREAMS

125 g (4½ oz) unsalted butter
115 g (4 oz/½ cup) caster (superfine) sugar
60 ml (2 fl oz/¼ cup) milk
185 g (6½ oz/1½ cups) self-raising flour
30 g (1 oz/¼ cup) custard powder or instant vanilla pudding mix
30 g (1 oz/⅓ cup) desiccated coconut
custard powder or instant vanilla pudding mix, extra

FILLING
75 g (2¾ oz) unsalted butter, softened
85 g (3 oz/⅔ cup) icing (confectioners') sugar
2 teaspoons milk
105 g (3¾ oz/⅓ cup) strawberry jam

MAKES 25

Preheat the oven to 180°C (350°F/Gas 4). Line two baking trays with baking paper. Cream the butter and sugar in a small bowl using electric beaters until light and fluffy. Add the milk and beat until combined. Sift the flour and custard powder and add to the bowl with the coconut. Mix to form a soft dough.

Roll 2 teaspoons of the mixture into balls. Place on the trays and press with a fork. Dip the fork in the extra custard powder occasionally to prevent it from sticking. Bake for 15–20 minutes, or until just golden. Transfer to a wire rack to cool completely before filling.

To make the filling, beat the butter and icing sugar in a small bowl using electric beaters until light and creamy. Beat in the milk. Spread one biscuit with ½ teaspoon of the filling and one with ½ teaspoon of jam, then press them together.

PREPARATION TIME: 30 MINUTES +   COOKING TIME: 20 MINUTES

CHOCOLATE WHEAT BISCUITS

125 g (4½ oz) butter
95 g (3½ oz/½ cup) soft brown sugar
60 ml (2 fl oz/¼ cup) milk
225 g (8 oz/1½ cups) wholemeal (whole-wheat) plain (all-purpose) flour
40 g (1½ oz/⅓ cup) self-raising flour
30 g (1 oz/⅓ cup) desiccated coconut
200 g (7 oz) dark chocolate

MAKES 25

Preheat the oven to 180°C (350°F/Gas 4). Brush two baking trays with melted butter or oil and line with baking paper. Beat the butter and sugar in a bowl using electric beaters until light and creamy. Add the milk and beat until combined.

Add the sifted flours and coconut. Using a flat-bladed knife, mix to a soft dough. Roll between two sheets of baking paper to 5 mm (¼ inch) thick. Using a 5 cm (2 inch) round cutter, cut rounds from the dough and place on the tray. Bake for 15–20 minutes, or until golden. Cool.

Melt the chocolate in a heatproof bowl over a saucepan of simmering water, making sure that the base of the bowl does not touch the water. Remove from the heat and allow to cool slightly. Spread evenly over the tops of the biscuits and allow to set.

PREPARATION TIME: 20 MINUTES +   COOKING TIME: 15–20 MINUTES

CHOCOLATE PEPPERMINT SLICE

85 g (3 oz/²/₃ cup) self-raising flour
30 g (1 oz/¹/₄ cup) unsweetened cocoa powder
45 g (1³/₄ oz/¹/₂ cup) desiccated coconut
55 g (2 oz/¹/₄ cup) sugar
140 g (5 oz) unsalted butter, melted
1 egg, lightly beaten

PEPPERMINT FILLING
185 g (6¹/₂ oz/1¹/₂ cups) icing (confectioners') sugar, sifted
30 g (1 oz) Copha (white vegetable shortening), melted
2 tablespoons milk
¹/₂ teaspoon natural peppermint extract

CHOCOLATE TOPPING
185 g (6¹/₂ oz) dark chocolate, chopped
30 g (1 oz) Copha (white vegetable shortening)

MAKES 24

Preheat the oven to 180°C (350°F/Gas 4). Lightly grease a shallow tin measuring 18 x 28 cm (7 x 11¹/₄ inches) and line with baking paper, leaving the paper hanging over on the two long sides.

Sift the flour and cocoa into a bowl. Stir in the coconut and sugar, then add the butter and egg and mix well. Press the mixture firmly into the tin. Bake for 15 minutes, then press down with the back of a spoon and leave to cool.

To make the filling, sift the icing sugar into a bowl. Stir in the Copha, milk and peppermint extract. Spread over the base and refrigerate for 5–10 minutes, or until firm.

To make the topping, put the chocolate and Copha in a heatproof bowl. Half-fill a saucepan with water, bring to the boil, then remove from the heat. Sit the bowl over the pan, making sure the base of the bowl does not touch the water. Stir occasionally until the chocolate and Copha have melted and combined. Spread evenly over the filling. Refrigerate the slice for 20 minutes, or until the topping is firm. Carefully lift the slice from the tin, using the paper as handles. Cut into pieces with a warm knife to give clean edges. Store in an airtight container in the refrigerator.

PREPARATION TIME: 25 MINUTES +   COOKING TIME: 20 MINUTES

PEANUT BISCUITS

185 g (6½ oz) unsalted butter, softened
370 g (13 oz/2 cups) soft brown sugar
140 g (5 oz) smooth peanut butter
1 teaspoon natural vanilla extract
1 egg
185 g (6½ oz/1½ cups) plain (all-purpose) flour
½ teaspoon baking powder
125 g (4½ oz/1¼ cups) rolled (porridge) oats
120 g (4¼ oz/¾ cup) peanuts

MAKES 30

Preheat the oven to 180°C (350°F/Gas 4). Line two baking trays with baking paper. Beat the butter, sugar, peanut butter and vanilla in a small bowl using electric beaters until light and creamy. Add the egg and beat until smooth. Transfer to a large bowl and mix in the combined sifted flour and baking powder. Fold in the oats and peanuts and mix until smooth. Chill until firm.

Roll heaped tablespoons of the mixture into balls and place on the trays, leaving room for spreading. Press down gently with a floured fork to make a crisscross pattern. Bake for 15–20 minutes, or until golden. Cool slightly on the trays before transferring to a wire rack to cool completely.

PREPARATION TIME: 30 MINUTES +   COOKING TIME: 20 MINUTES

HARD CARAMELS

220 g (7¾ oz/1 cup) sugar
90 g (3¼ oz) unsalted butter
2 tablespoons golden syrup or dark corn syrup
80 ml (2½ fl oz/⅓ cup) liquid glucose
90 ml (3 fl oz) condensed milk
250 g (9 oz) dark chocolate, chopped

MAKES 49

Grease the base and sides of a 20 cm (8 inch) square cake tin, then line with baking paper and grease the paper. Combine the sugar, butter, syrup, glucose and milk in a heavy-based saucepan. Stir over medium heat without boiling until the butter has melted and the sugar has dissolved completely. Brush the sugar crystals from the sides of the saucepan with a wet pastry brush. Bring to the boil, reduce the heat slightly and boil, stirring, for about 10–15 minutes, or until a teaspoon of mixture dropped into cold water reaches hard ball stage (forming a firm ball that holds its shape). If using a sugar thermometer, the mixture must reach 122°C (250°F). Remove from the heat immediately. Pour into the tin and leave to cool. While the caramel is still warm, mark into 49 squares with an oiled knife. When cold, cut through completely into squares.

Line two baking trays with foil. Place the chocolate in a small heatproof bowl. Bring a saucepan of water to the boil, then remove the saucepan from the heat. Sit the bowl over the saucepan, making sure the base of the bowl does not touch the water. Stir until the chocolate has melted. Remove from the heat and cool slightly. Using two forks, dip the caramels one at a time into the chocolate to coat. Lift out, drain the excess chocolate, then place on the trays and leave to set.

PREPARATION TIME: 25 MINUTES +   COOKING TIME: 20 MINUTES

CITRUS BISCUITS

125 g (4½ oz) unsalted butter, softened
115 g (4 oz/½ cup) caster (superfine) sugar
2 teaspoons grated orange or lemon zest
60 ml (2 fl oz/¼ cup) milk
185 g (6½ oz/1½ cups) self-raising flour
60 g (2¼ oz/½ cup) custard powder or instant vanilla pudding mix

ICING
250 g (9 oz/2 cups) sifted icing (confectioners') sugar
20 g (¾ oz) unsalted butter, softened
1 tablespoon lemon or orange juice

MAKES 30

Line two baking trays with baking paper or lightly grease with some melted butter. Preheat the oven to 210°C (415°F/Gas 6–7) and check the racks are near the centre.

Cut the butter into cubes, then cream with the caster sugar and orange or lemon zest in a small bowl using electric beaters, or by hand, until light and creamy. Scrape down the side of the bowl occasionally with a spatula. The mixture should look pale and be quite smooth. The sugar should be almost dissolved. Add the milk and beat until combined. Add the flour and custard powder and use a flat-bladed knife to bring to a soft dough.

Rotate the bowl as you work and use a cutting action to incorporate the dry ingredients. Don't overwork the dough or you will end up with tough biscuits (cookies). Roll level teaspoons into balls and place on the trays, leaving 5 cm (2 inches) between each biscuit. Flatten the balls lightly with your fingertips, then press with a fork. The biscuits should be about 5 cm (2 inches) in diameter. Bake for 15–20 minutes, or until lightly golden. Cool on the trays for 3 minutes before transferring to a wire rack to cool completely.

To make the icing (frosting), combine the icing sugar, butter and lemon or orange juice in a small bowl, then spread over the tops of the biscuits.

PREPARATION TIME: 20 MINUTES   COOKING TIME: 20 MINUTES

NOTE: Store in an airtight container for up to a week. To freeze, place in freezer bags and seal, label and date. Un-iced cooked biscuits can be frozen for up to 2 months. After thawing, refresh them in a 180°C (350°F/Gas 4) oven for a few minutes, then cool and decorate, as desired, before serving.

GINGER SHORTBREAD

250 g (9 oz) unsalted butter, softened
60 g (2¼ oz/½ cup) icing (confectioners')
sugar
250 g (9 oz/2 cups) plain (all-purpose)
flour
1 teaspoon ground ginger
70 g (2½ oz/⅓ cup) chopped crystallized
ginger

MAKES 12

Preheat the oven to 150°C (300°F/Gas 2). Line a 23 cm (9 inch) round or square tin or a baking tray with baking paper.

Cream the butter and sugar in a small bowl using electric beaters until light and fluffy. Sift the flour into the bowl with the ground ginger. Add the chopped ginger and mix with a flat-bladed knife, using a cutting action, to form a soft dough. Gently gather together and press into the tin, or shape into a round about 1 cm (½ inch) thick on the baking tray. Pierce all over with a fork and score into 12 wedges.

Bake for 40–45 minutes, or until lightly golden. While still warm, cut into wedges. Cool in the tin or on the tray for about 3 minutes before transferring to a wire rack to cool completely. When cold, store in an airtight container.

PREPARATION TIME: 25 MINUTES   COOKING TIME: 45 MINUTES

APPLE CINNAMON MUFFINS

400 g (14 oz) tinned pie apple
310 g (11 oz/2½ cups) self-raising flour
2 teaspoons ground cinnamon
125 g (4½ oz/⅔ cup) soft brown sugar
350 ml (12 fl oz) milk
2 eggs
1 teaspoon natural vanilla extract
150 g (5½ oz) unsalted butter, melted and
cooled
60 g (2¼ oz/½ cup) walnuts, finely
chopped

MAKES 12

Preheat the oven to 200°C (400°F/Gas 6). Lightly grease a 12-hole standard muffin tin or line the muffin tin with paper cases. Place the pie apple in a bowl and break it up with a knife.

Sift the flour and cinnamon into a bowl and add the sugar. Make a well in the centre. Whisk together the milk, eggs and vanilla and pour into the well. Add the completely cooled melted butter.

Fold the mixture gently with a metal spoon until just combined. Add the apple and stir through. Do not overmix — the batter will still be slightly lumpy.

Fill each muffin hole with the mixture (the holes will be quite full, but don't worry because these muffins don't rise as much as some) and sprinkle with the walnuts. Bake for 20–25 minutes, or until golden and a skewer inserted into the centre of a muffin comes out clean. Leave the muffins in the tin for a couple of minutes to cool. Gently loosen each muffin with a flat-bladed knife before turning out onto a wire rack. Serve warm or at room temperature.

PREPARATION TIME: 15 MINUTES   COOKING TIME: 25 MINUTES

Ginger shortbread

STRAWBERRY AND PASSIONFRUIT MUFFINS

215 g (7³/₄ oz/1³/₄ cups) self-raising flour
1 teaspoon baking powder
¹/₂ teaspoon bicarbonate of soda
(baking soda)
55 g (2 oz/¹/₄ cup) caster (superfine) sugar
175 g (6 oz/1 cup) chopped strawberries
125 g (4¹/₂ oz) tinned (or fresh)
passionfruit pulp
1 egg
185 ml (6 fl oz/³/₄ cup) milk
60 g (2¹/₂ oz) unsalted butter, melted
whipped cream, fresh strawberry halves
and icing (confectioners') sugar, to serve
(optional)

MAKES 12

Preheat the oven to 210°C (415°F/Gas 6–7). Lightly grease a 12-hole standard muffin tin, or line the muffin tin with paper cases.

Sift the flour, baking powder, bicarbonate of soda, sugar and a pinch of salt into a bowl. Add the strawberries and stir to combine. Make a well in the centre.

Add the passionfruit pulp and the combined egg and milk. Pour the melted butter into the flour mixture all at once and lightly stir with a fork until just combined. Do not overbeat — the batter will still be slightly lumpy.

Divide the mixture evenly among the holes — fill each hole to about three-quarters full. Bake for 10–15 minutes, or until golden and a skewer inserted into the centre of a muffin comes out clean. Leave the muffins in the tin for a couple of minutes to cool. Gently loosen each muffin with a flat-bladed knife before turning out onto a wire rack to cool.

Top the muffins with softened, sweetened cream cheese or whipped cream and fresh strawberry halves and sprinkle with icing sugar, if desired.

PREPARATION TIME: 20 MINUTES   COOKING TIME: 10–15 MINUTES

CHOCOLATE CLUSTERS

125 g (4^1/$_2$ oz) dark chocolate melts
125 g (4^1/$_2$ oz) white chocolate melts
125 g (4^1/$_2$ oz/^{2}/$_3$ cup) dried mixed fruit
125 g (4^1/$_2$ oz) glacé ginger, chopped
30 g (1 oz) dark chocolate melts, extra, melted
30 g (1 oz) white chocolate melts, extra, melted

MAKES ABOUT 40

Put the dark chocolate in a heatproof bowl. Bring a saucepan of water to the boil, then remove from the heat. Sit the bowl over the pan, making sure the base of the bowl does not touch the water. Stir occasionally until the chocolate has melted. Cool slightly. Repeat with the white chocolate.

Stir the mixed fruit into the dark chocolate. Combine the ginger with the white chocolate. Drop spoonfuls of the mixtures onto foil-lined trays, and leave to set at room temperature. Drizzle with the extra melted chocolate.

PREPARATION TIME: 35 MINUTES   COOKING TIME: NIL

CHOCOLATE CUPS WITH CARAMEL

150 g (5^1/$_2$ oz/1 cup) dark chocolate melts
80 g (2^3/$_4$ oz) Mars® bar, chopped
60 ml (2 fl oz/^{1}/$_4$ cup) pouring (whipping) cream
50 g (1^3/$_4$ oz/^{1}/$_3$ cup) white chocolate melts

MAKES 24

Place the dark chocolate in a small heatproof bowl. Bring a small saucepan of water to the boil and remove from the heat. Sit the bowl over the pan, making sure the base of the bowl does not touch the water. Stir occasionally until the chocolate has melted and the mixture is smooth.

Brush a thin layer of chocolate inside 24 small foil confectionery cases. Stand the cases upside-down on a wire rack to set. (Return the bowl of remaining chocolate to the pan of steaming water for later use.)

Combine the Mars® bar and cream in a small saucepan and stir over low heat until the chocolate has melted and the mixture is smooth. Transfer to a bowl and leave until just starting to set, then spoon into each foil case leaving about 3 mm (^{1}/$_8$ inch) of space at the top.

Spoon the reserved melted chocolate into the caramel cases and allow the chocolate to set. Melt the white chocolate in the same way as the dark chocolate. Place in a small paper piping (icing) bag and drizzle patterns over the cups. Carefully peel away the foil when the chocolate has set.

PREPARATION TIME: 40 MINUTES +   COOKING TIME: 10 MINUTES

NOTE: Caramel cups can be made up to 3 days ahead. Ensure the chocolate is set before piping the white chocolate on the top.

CHOCOLATE TARTS

PASTRY
155 g (5½ oz/1¼ cups) plain (all-purpose) flour
75 g (2¾ oz) unsalted butter, chopped
55 g (2 oz/¼ cup) caster (superfine) sugar
2 egg yolks

250 g (9 oz) dark chocolate, finely chopped
250 ml (9 fl oz/1 cup) pouring (whipping) cream
1 tablespoon orange-flavoured liqueur
1 orange
115 g (4 oz/½ cup) caster (superfine) sugar, extra
unsweetened cocoa powder, to dust

MAKES ABOUT 45

Lightly grease two 12-hole tartlet tins. To make the pastry, sift the flour into a large bowl and add the butter. Rub in with your fingertips until the mixture resembles fine breadcrumbs. Stir in the sugar. Make a well in the centre and add the egg yolks and up to 2 tablespoons water. Mix with a flat-bladed knife using a cutting action, until the mixture comes together in beads. Gather together and lift out onto a lightly floured work surface. Press into a ball and flatten slightly into a disc. Wrap in plastic and refrigerate for 20 minutes.

Preheat the oven to 180°C (350°F/Gas 4). Roll the dough between two sheets of baking paper and cut rounds with a 5 cm (2 inch) cutter. Press into the tins.

Bake for about 10 minutes, or until lightly browned. Remove from the tins and cool. Repeat to use all the pastry. Allow to cool.

Put the chocolate in a heatproof bowl. Bring the cream to the boil in a small saucepan and pour over the chocolate. Leave for 1 minute, then stir until the chocolate has melted. Stir in the liqueur. Allow to set, stirring occasionally until thick.

Meanwhile, thinly peel the orange, avoiding the bitter white pith, and cut the peel into short thin strips. Combine the extra sugar, peel and 125 ml (4 fl oz/½ cup) water in a small saucepan, stir over heat until the sugar has dissolved, then simmer for about 5–10 minutes, or until thick and syrupy. Remove the peel with tongs, drain on baking paper and allow to cool.

Spoon the chocolate mixture into a piping (icing) bag fitted with a 1 cm (½ inch) plain piping nozzle. Pipe three small blobs of mixture into the pastry case, pulling up as you pipe so the mixture forms a point. Dust with cocoa, decorate with the orange zest and refrigerate until ready to serve.

PREPARATION TIME: 40 MINUTES +   COOKING TIME: 30 MINUTES

AMANDINE

100 g (3½ oz) hazelnuts
120 g (4¼ oz) almonds
185 g (6½ oz/1 cup) soft brown sugar
360 g (12¾ oz/1⅔ cups) sugar
175 g (6 oz/½ cup) honey
1 lemon, halved
115 g (4 oz) unsalted butter

SERVES 4–6

Preheat the oven to 170°C (325°F/Gas 3). Spread the hazelnuts on a baking tray and roast for about 5 minutes, or until their skins crack. Remove from the oven and reduce the temperature to 150°C (300°F/Gas 2). Wrap them in a tea towel (dish towel), rub together to dislodge their skins and allow to cool. Put the skinned nuts into a food processor. Place the almonds on the baking tray and bake for 6 minutes, or until browned. Allow to cool, then transfer the almonds to the processor. Chop the nuts until they look like little pebbles.

Grease a large baking tray. Place 125 ml (4 fl oz/½ cup) water in a heavy-based saucepan with the sugars and honey. Bring to the boil, stirring only until the sugars have melted. Remove any seeds visible in the lemon halves and squeeze 2–3 drops of juice into the boiling syrup. Reserve the lemons. Simmer the syrup for 8–10 minutes, or until it reaches 150°C (300°F). Stir in the butter and, when melted, add the nuts. Pour onto the prepared surface and, using the lemon halves as tools, spread and smooth the toffee out to a 5 mm (¼ inch) thick sheet. Leave to cool and set hard. Crack up into pieces for serving.

PREPARATION TIME: 25 MINUTES   COOKING TIME: 30 MINUTES

CHOCOLATE MERINGUE KISSES

2 egg whites, at room temperature
115 g (4 oz/½ cup) caster (superfine) sugar
¼ teaspoon ground cinnamon

FILLING
125 g (4½ oz) dark chocolate melts or buttons
90 g (3¼ oz/⅓ cup) sour cream

MAKES 25

Preheat the oven to 150°C (300°F/Gas 2). Line two baking trays with baking paper. Beat the egg whites using electric beaters in a small, clean, dry bowl until soft peaks form. Add the sugar gradually, beating thoroughly after each addition until stiffened and glossy peaks form. Add the cinnamon and beat until just combined. Transfer the mixture to a piping (icing) bag fitted with a 1 cm (½ inch) fluted nozzle. Pipe small stars of 1.5 cm (⅝ inch) diameter onto the trays, 3 cm (1¼ inches) apart. Bake for 30 minutes, or until pale and crisp. Turn off the oven. Leave the meringues to cool in the oven with the door ajar.

To make the filling, place the chocolate and sour cream in a small heatproof bowl. Bring a saucepan of water to the boil, remove from the heat and sit the bowl over the pan, making sure the base of the bowl does not sit in the water. Stir occasionally until the chocolate has melted. Remove from the heat and cool slightly. Sandwich the meringues together with the chocolate filling.

PREPARATION TIME: 20 MINUTES +   COOKING TIME: 40 MINUTES

CHOCOLATE PEPPERMINT CREAMS

65 g (2¹/₂ oz) unsalted butter
55 g (2 oz/¹/₄ cup) caster (superfine) sugar
60 g (2¹/₄ oz/¹/₂ cup) plain (all-purpose) flour
40 g (1¹/₂ oz/¹/₃ cup) self-raising flour
2 tablespoons unsweetened cocoa powder
2 tablespoons milk

PEPPERMINT CREAM
1 egg white
215 g (7³/₄ oz/1³/₄ cups) icing (confectioners') sugar, sifted
2–3 drops natural peppermint extract or oil, to taste

CHOCOLATE TOPPING
150 g (5¹/₂ oz) dark chocolate, chopped
150 g (5¹/₂ oz/1 cup) dark chocolate melts

MAKES 20

Preheat the oven to 180°C (350°F/Gas 4). Line two baking trays with baking paper.

Cream the butter and sugar in a small bowl using electric beaters until light and fluffy. Add the sifted flours and cocoa alternately with the milk. Mix with a flat-bladed knife, using a cutting action, until the mixture forms a soft dough. Turn out onto a floured surface and gather together into a rough ball. Cut the dough in half. Roll each half between two sheets of baking paper to 2 mm (¹/₁₆ inch) thick. Slide onto a tray and refrigerate for 15 minutes, or until firm. Cut the dough into rounds using a 4 cm (1¹/₂ inch) round cutter, re-rolling the dough scraps and cutting more rounds. Place on the trays, allowing room for spreading. Bake for 10 minutes, or until firm. Transfer to a wire rack to cool completely.

To make the peppermint cream, put the egg white in a small, clean, dry bowl. Beat in the icing sugar, 2 tablespoons at a time, using electric beaters on low speed. Add more icing sugar, if necessary, until a soft dough forms. Turn the dough onto a surface dusted with icing sugar and knead in enough icing sugar so that the dough is not sticky. Knead in the peppermint extract.

Roll a teaspoon of peppermint cream into a ball, and flatten slightly. Sandwich between two chocolate biscuits, pressing together to spread the peppermint to the edges. Repeat with the remaining filling and chocolate biscuits, keeping the filling covered as you work.

To make the topping, put the chopped chocolate and the chocolate melts in a heatproof bowl. Half-fill a saucepan with water and bring to the boil. Remove from the heat and place the bowl over the pan, making sure the base of the bowl does not touch the water. Stir occasionally until the chocolate is melted. Remove from the heat and allow to cool slightly. Use a fork to dip the biscuits into the chocolate and allow any excess to drain away. Place on a tray lined with baking paper to set.

PREPARATION TIME: 40 MINUTES +   COOKING TIME: 20 MINUTES

WHITE CAKE TRUFFLES

250 g (9 oz) Madeira cake crumbs
2 tablespoons chopped glacé orange peel
or glacé apricots
1 tablespoon apricot jam
2 tablespoons pouring (whipping) cream
100 g (3½ oz) white chocolate, melted
gold leaf, to decorate (optional)

CHOCOLATE COATING
150 g (5½ oz) white chocolate, chopped
20 g (¾ oz) Copha (white vegetable
shortening), chopped

MAKES ABOUT 25

Line a baking tray with foil. Combine the cake crumbs in a bowl with the chopped peel or apricots, jam, cream and melted chocolate. Mix until smooth, then roll into balls using 2 teaspoons of mixture for each ball.

To make the chocolate coating, combine the chocolate and shortening in a heatproof bowl. Bring a saucepan of water to the boil, remove from the heat and sit the bowl over the pan, making sure the base of the bowl does not touch the water. Stir occasionally until the chocolate and shortening have melted. Dip the balls in chocolate, wipe the excess off on the edge of the bowl and leave them to set on the tray. Decorate with gold leaf, if desired.

PREPARATION TIME: 25 MINUTES   COOKING TIME: 5 MINUTES

NOTES: For decorating, you can buy 24-carat edible gold leaf from speciality art shops or cake decorating suppliers.
    These truffles can be made up to 2 weeks ahead.

RICH CHOCOLATE TRUFFLES

185 ml (6 fl oz/¾ cup) thick
(double/heavy) cream
400 g (14 oz) dark chocolate, grated
70 g (2½ oz) unsalted butter, chopped
2 tablespoons Cointreau
dark unsweetened cocoa powder, for
rolling

MAKES ABOUT 30

Place the cream in a small saucepan and bring to the boil. Remove from the heat and stir in the chocolate until it is completely melted. Add the butter and stir until melted. Stir in the Cointreau. Transfer to a large bowl, cover and refrigerate for several hours or overnight, or until firm enough to roll.

Quickly roll tablespoons of the mixture into balls, and refrigerate until firm. Roll the balls in the cocoa, shake off any excess and return to the refrigerator. Serve at room temperature.

PREPARATION TIME: 40 MINUTES +   COOKING TIME: 5 MINUTES

NOTE: The truffle mixture can be made and rolled up to 2 weeks ahead. You will need to roll the balls in cocoa again close to serving time.

PRALINE TRIANGLES

60 g (2¼ oz/½ cup) slivered almonds
115 g (4 oz/½ cup) caster (superfine) sugar
150 g (5½ oz) dark chocolate, chopped
40 g (1½ oz) unsalted butter
60 ml (2 fl oz/¼ cup) pouring (whipping) cream
80 g (2¾ oz) blanched almonds, toasted
200 g (7 oz) dark chocolate, melted
50 g (1¾ oz) white chocolate (optional)

MAKES 36

Line a baking tray with foil and brush lightly with oil. Line a 10 x 20 cm (4 x 8 inch) loaf (bar) tin with foil.

Combine the almonds and sugar in a small saucepan and place over low heat. Watch carefully, without stirring, for 3-5 minutes, until the sugar is melted and golden. (Swirl the pan slightly to dissolve the sugar.) Pour onto the tray and leave until set and completely cold. Break the praline into chunks, place in a plastic bag and crush with a rolling pin, or chop in a food processor until crumbly.

Put the chopped chocolate in a heatproof bowl. Combine the butter and cream in a small saucepan and stir over low heat until the butter melts. Bring to the boil, then remove from the heat. Pour the hot cream mixture over the chocolate. Leave for 2 minutes, then stir until the chocolate is smooth. Cool slightly, then stir in the crushed praline.

Spread the mixture into the loaf tin and smooth the surface. Tap gently on the bench to level. Cover with plastic wrap, then refrigerate for 1 hour, or until set. Lift from the tin, peel away the foil and cut into 36 small triangles.

Line a tray with foil. Press a whole toasted almond onto each triangle. Using two forks, dip the triangles one at a time into the melted dark chocolate to coat. Lift out, drain off the excess chocolate and place on the tray to set. Pipe with white chocolate to decorate, if desired.

PREPARATION TIME: 40 MINUTES +   COOKING TIME: 10 MINUTES

NOTE: Refrigerate in warm weather.

BEIGNETS DE FRUITS

3 granny smith or golden delicious apples
70 g (2¹/₂ oz) raisins
60 ml (2 fl oz/¹/₄ cup) Calvados or rum
1¹/₂ tablespoons caster (superfine) sugar
oil, for frying
2 tablespoons plain (all-purpose) flour, to coat
icing (confectioners') sugar, to dust

BATTER
1 egg, separated
70 ml (2¹/₄ fl oz) warm beer
60 g (2¹/₄ oz/¹/₂ cup) plain (all-purpose) flour
1 teaspoon oil

Peel and core the apples and cut into 1 cm (¹/₂ inch) cubes. Place in a bowl with the raisins, Calvados and sugar and marinate for 3 hours.

To make the batter, beat the egg yolk and beer together in a large bowl. Blend in the flour, oil and a pinch of salt. Stir until smooth. The batter will be very thick at this stage. Cover and leave in a warm place for 1 hour.

Pour the oil into a large saucepan to a depth of 10 cm (4 inches) and heat to 170°C (325°F), or until a cube of bread dropped into the oil browns in 20 seconds. Add 1¹/₂ tablespoons of the Calvados marinade to the batter and stir until smooth. Whisk the egg white until stiff and gently fold into the batter. Drain the apples and raisins, toss with the flour to coat, then lightly fold them through the batter. Carefully lower heaped tablespoons of batter into the oil in batches and fry for 1–2 minutes, until the fritters are golden on both sides. Remove with a slotted spoon and drain on paper towels. Keep them warm. Dust with icing sugar and serve.

SERVES 4   PREPARATION TIME: 25 MINUTES +   COOKING TIME: 10 MINUTES

DOUBLE CHOCOLATE MUFFINS

250 g (9 oz/2 cups) plain (all-purpose) flour
2¹/₂ teaspoons baking powder
30 g (1 oz/¹/₄ cup) unsweetened cocoa powder
2 tablespoons caster (superfine) sugar
175 g (6 oz/1 cup) dark chocolate chips
1 egg, lightly beaten
125 g (4¹/₂ oz/¹/₂ cup) sour cream
185 ml (6 fl oz/³/₄ cup) milk
90 g (3¹/₄ oz) unsalted butter, melted

Preheat the oven to 180°C (350°F/Gas 4). Lightly grease a 6-hole large muffin tin. Sift the flour, baking powder and cocoa into a large mixing bowl. Add the sugar and the chocolate chips and stir to mix through. Make a well in the centre. Add the combined egg, sour cream, milk and melted butter all at once and stir with a fork until just combined. Do not overbeat — the batter will still be slightly lumpy.

Divide the mixture evenly among the holes — fill each hole to about three-quarters full. Bake for 12–15 minutes, or until firm. Leave in the tin for a couple of minutes to cool. Gently loosen each muffin with a flat-bladed knife before turning out onto a wire rack.

MAKES 6   PREPARATION TIME: 15 MINUTES   COOKING TIME: 15 MINUTES

TEARDROP CHOCOLATE CHERRY MOUSSE CUPS

200 g (7 oz/1⅓ cups) dark chocolate melts or buttons
150 g (5½ oz/¾ cup) stoneless black cherries, well drained

CHOCOLATE MOUSSE
60 g (2¼ oz) dark chocolate, melted
1 tablespoon pouring (whipping) cream
1 egg yolk
½ teaspoon powdered gelatine
80 ml (2½ fl oz/⅓ cup) pouring (whipping) cream, extra
1 egg white

MAKES ABOUT 24

Cut glossy contact into 24 rectangles measuring 4 x 11 cm (1½ x 4¼ inches). Line a tray with baking paper. Place the chocolate melts in a small heatproof bowl. Bring a small saucepan of water to the boil and remove from the heat. Sit the bowl over the pan, making sure the base of the bowl does not touch the water. Stir occasionally until the chocolate has melted and the mixture is smooth. Using a palette or flat-bladed knife, spread a little of the chocolate over one of the contact rectangles. Just before the chocolate starts to set, bring the short edges together to form a teardrop shape. (Leave the contact attached.) Hold together with your fingers until the shape holds by itself and will stand up. Repeat with some of the remaining chocolate and rectangles. (The chocolate will need to be re-melted several times. To do this, place the bowl over steaming water again.)

Spoon about 1½ teaspoons of the remaining chocolate on the tray and spread into an oval about 5 cm (2 inches) long. Sit a teardrop in the centre of it and press down gently. Repeat with the remaining teardrops. Allow to almost set. Using a small sharp knife or scalpel, cut around the outer edge of each teardrop. Allow the cups to set completely before lifting away from the baking paper. Carefully break away the excess chocolate from the bases to form a neat edge on the base. Carefully peel away the contact. Set the cups aside. Cut the cherries into quarters and drain on crumpled paper towels.

To make the mousse, mix the chocolate, cream and egg yolk in a bowl until smooth. Sprinkle the gelatine in an even layer over 2 teaspoons water in a small heatproof bowl and leave until spongy. Bring a small saucepan of water to the boil, remove from the heat and place the bowl containing the gelatine mixture over the pan. The water should come halfway up the side of the bowl. Stir the gelatine until clear and dissolved. Stir into the chocolate mixture. Working quickly, so the gelatine does not set, beat the extra cream using electric beaters until soft peaks form, then fold into the chocolate. Using electric beaters, beat the egg white in a clean dry bowl until soft peaks form. Fold into the chocolate.

Place a few pieces of cherry inside each teardrop cup. Spoon the chocolate mousse over the cherries. (Fill to slightly over the brim as the mousse will drop during setting.) Chill until set.

PREPARATION TIME: 1 HOUR +   COOKING TIME: NIL

HONEY BISCUITS

210 g (7¹/₂ oz/1²/₃ cups) plain (all-purpose) flour

1 teaspoon baking powder

1 tablespoon finely grated orange zest

1 teaspoon ground cinnamon

60 g (2¹/₄ oz/¹/₂ cup) walnuts, finely chopped

60 g (2¹/₄ oz) unsalted butter, softened

55 g (2 oz/¹/₄ cup) caster (superfine) sugar

60 ml (2 fl oz/¹/₄ cup) olive oil

60 ml (2 fl oz/¹/₄ cup) orange juice

SYRUP

75 g (2³/₄ oz) caster (superfine) sugar

2 tablespoons runny honey

1 teaspoon ground cinnamon

2 tablespoons orange juice

MAKES 20

Preheat the oven to 180°C (350°F/Gas 4). Line a baking tray with baking paper. Sift the flour and baking powder into a bowl. Mix in the zest, cinnamon and half the walnuts. Cream the butter and sugar in another bowl using electric beaters until pale and fluffy. Mix the oil and orange juice and add, a little at a time, to the butter and sugar mixture, whisking constantly.

Mix the flour in two batches into the butter mixture, then bring the dough together with your hands. Shape tablespoons of dough into balls and place on the tray. Flatten slightly and bake for 20–25 minutes, until golden. Cool on the tray.

To make the syrup, mix all the ingredients with 60 ml (2 fl oz/¹/₄ cup) water and the remaining walnuts in a small saucepan. Bring to the boil over medium heat until the sugar dissolves, then reduce the heat to low and simmer for 10 minutes. The syrup will thicken. Using a slotted spoon, dip a few biscuits at a time in the hot syrup. Use another spoon to baste them, then transfer to a plate.

PREPARATION TIME: 20 MINUTES +   COOKING TIME: 35 MINUTES

CAPPUCCINO BROWNIES

150 g (5¹/₂ oz) unsalted butter

125 g (4¹/₂ oz) dark chocolate

3 eggs

345 g (12 oz/1¹/₂ cups) caster (superfine) sugar

1 teaspoon natural vanilla extract

125 g (4¹/₂ oz/1 cup) plain (all-purpose) flour

30 g (1 oz/¹/₄ cup) unsweetened cocoa powder

2 tablespoons instant coffee powder

1 litre (35 fl oz/4 cups) vanilla ice cream

1 teaspoon drinking chocolate

SERVES 6

Preheat the oven to 180°C (350°F/Gas 4). Grease an 18 x 28 cm (7 x 11¹/₄ inch) shallow baking tin and line the base with baking paper, extending over two sides. Place the butter and chocolate in a small heatproof bowl. Bring a saucepan of water to the boil, remove from the heat and sit the bowl over the pan, making sure the base of the bowl does not touch the water. Stir until melted and smooth. Remove from the pan and allow to cool slightly.

In a large bowl, whisk the eggs, sugar and vanilla together. Whisk in the chocolate mixture, then stir in the sifted flour, cocoa and coffee powder. Do not overbeat. Pour into the tin and bake for 40 minutes. Cool the brownie in the tin until warm.

Lift from the tin, using the paper as handles. Using an 8 cm (3¹/₄ inch) round biscuit (cookie) cutter, cut out six rounds while the brownie is still warm. Place each round on a serving plate, top with three small scoops of ice cream and dust lightly with drinking chocolate. Serve immediately.

PREPARATION TIME: 20 MINUTES   COOKING TIME: 40 MINUTES

Honey biscuits

LUMBERJACK CAKE

200 g (7 oz) fresh dates, stoned and chopped
1 teaspoon bicarbonate of soda (baking soda)
125 g (4$\frac{1}{2}$ oz) unsalted butter, softened
230 g (8$\frac{1}{2}$ oz/1 cup) caster (superfine) sugar
1 egg
1 teaspoon natural vanilla extract
2 granny smith apples, peeled, cored and grated
125 g (4$\frac{1}{2}$ oz/1 cup) plain (all-purpose) flour
60 g (2$\frac{1}{4}$ oz/$\frac{1}{2}$ cup) self-raising flour
icing (confectioners') sugar (optional), to dust

TOPPING
75 g (2$\frac{3}{4}$ oz) unsalted butter
95 g (3$\frac{1}{2}$ oz/$\frac{1}{2}$ cup) soft brown sugar
80 ml (2$\frac{1}{2}$ fl oz/$\frac{1}{3}$ cup) milk
60 g (2$\frac{1}{4}$ oz/1 cup) shredded coconut

SERVES 8

Grease a 20 cm (8 inch) round spring-form cake tin and line the base with baking paper. Preheat the oven to 180°C (350°F/Gas 4).

Put the dates in a small saucepan with 250 ml (9 fl oz/1 cup) water and bring to the boil. Stir in the bicarbonate of soda, then remove from the heat. Set aside until just warm.

Cream the butter and sugar in a small bowl using electric beaters until light and fluffy. Add the egg and vanilla and beat until combined. Stir in the date mixture and the apple, then fold in the sifted flours until just combined and almost smooth. Spoon into the tin and smooth the surface. Bake for 40 minutes.

To make the topping, combine all the ingredients in a small saucepan and stir over low heat until the butter has melted and the ingredients are well combined. Remove the cake from the oven and carefully spread the topping over the cake. Return the cake to the oven for 20–30 minutes, or until the topping is golden and a skewer inserted into the centre of the cake comes out clean.

Remove from the oven and leave the cake in the tin to cool completely, then turn out and place on a serving plate. The cake can be dusted with icing sugar just before serving.

PREPARATION TIME: 30 MINUTES   COOKING TIME: 1 HOUR 15 MINUTES

FLOURLESS CHOCOLATE CAKE

250 g (9 oz) dark chocolate, chopped
100 g (3^1/$_2$ oz) caster (superfine) sugar
100 g (3^1/$_2$ oz) unsalted butter, cubed
1 tablespoon coffee-flavoured liqueur
125 g (4^1/$_2$ oz) ground hazelnuts
5 eggs, separated
icing (confectioners') sugar, to dust

SERVES 10–12

Preheat the oven to 180°C (350°F/Gas 4). Grease a 23 cm (9 inch) spring-form cake tin and line the base with baking paper. Place the chocolate, sugar, butter and liqueur in a heatproof bowl. Bring a small saucepan of water to the boil, then reduce the heat to a gentle simmer. Sit the bowl over the saucepan, making sure the base of the bowl does not touch the water. Stir occasionally to ensure even melting. When fully melted, remove from the heat and mix thoroughly.

Transfer the chocolate mixture to a large bowl. Stir in the hazelnuts, then beat in the egg yolks, one at a time, mixing well after each addition. In a dry bowl, whisk the egg whites until they form medium stiff peaks. Stir a tablespoonful of the whisked egg whites into the chocolate, then gently fold in the rest using a large metal spoon or rubber spatula.

Pour the mixture into the tin and bake for 50–60 minutes, or until a skewer inserted into the centre of the cake comes out clean. Leave to cool completely in the tin before turning out and dusting with icing sugar.

PREPARATION TIME: 20 MINUTES   COOKING TIME: 1 HOUR 5 MINUTES

STRAWBERRY SWISS ROLL

caster (superfine) sugar, to sprinkle
3 eggs, separated
115 g (4 oz/^{1}/$_2$ cup) caster (superfine) sugar, extra
90 g (3^1/$_4$ oz/^{3}/$_4$ cup) self-raising flour, sifted
185 ml (6 fl oz/^{3}/$_4$ cup) pouring (whipping) cream
1 tablespoon caster (superfine) sugar, extra
160 g (5^3/$_4$ oz/^{1}/$_2$ cup) strawberry jam
250 g (9 oz/1^2/$_3$ cups) strawberries, quartered

SERVES 6–8

Preheat the oven to 200°C (400°F/Gas 6). Sprinkle a tablespoon of sugar over a piece of baking paper 30 x 35 cm (12 x 14 inches), resting on a tea towel (dish towel). Brush a 25 x 30 cm (10 x 12 inch) Swiss roll tin (jelly roll tin) with oil or melted butter and line with baking paper. Beat the egg whites in a clean, dry bowl until soft peaks form. Gradually add the extra ^{1}/$_2$ cup sugar and beat until dissolved. Beat in the lightly beaten egg yolks until thick.

Fold in the flour and 2 tablespoons hot water. Spread into the tin and bake for 8–10 minutes, or until firm and golden. Turn out onto the sugared paper and peel the paper from the base. Using the tea towel as a guide, roll up loosely from the narrow end. Leave for 20 minutes, or until cooled, then unroll. (This prevents the sponge cracking when rolled with filling.) Beat the cream and extra tablespoon of sugar until soft peaks form. Spread the roll with jam and top with cream and strawberries. Re-roll and chill.

PREPARATION TIME: 25 MINUTES +   COOKING TIME: 10 MINUTES

Flourless chocolate cake

HONEY CREAM ROLL

90 g (3¹/4 oz/³/4 cup) self-raising flour
2 teaspoons ground mixed (pumpkin pie) spice
3 eggs
125 g (4¹/2 oz/²/3 cup) soft brown sugar
25 g (1 oz/¹/4 cup) desiccated coconut

HONEY CREAM
125 g (4¹/2 oz) unsalted butter, softened
40 g (1¹/2 oz/¹/3 cup) icing (confectioners') sugar
2 tablespoons honey

SERVES 8–10

Preheat the oven to 190°C (375°F/Gas 5). Lightly grease a 2 x 25 x 30 cm (³/4 x 10 x 12 inch) Swiss roll tin (jelly roll tin) and line the base with baking paper, extending over the two long sides. Sift the flour and mixed spice three times onto a sheet of baking paper. Beat the eggs in a large bowl using electric beaters for 5 minutes, or until thick, frothy and pale. Add the sugar gradually, beating constantly until the sugar has dissolved and the mixture is pale and glossy. Using a metal spoon, fold in the flour quickly and lightly. Spread into the tin and smooth the surface. Bake for 10–12 minutes, or until the cake is lightly golden and springy to touch.

Meanwhile, place a clean tea towel (dish towel) on a work surface, cover with baking paper and sprinkle the paper with coconut. Turn the cooked cake out onto the coconut. Using the tea towel as a guide, carefully roll up the cake, along with the paper, from the short side. Leave until cool.

To make the honey cream, beat all the ingredients in a bowl using electric beaters until the mixture is light and creamy and the sugar has dissolved. Unroll the cake and discard the paper. Spread with the honey cream and re-roll. Trim the ends with a knife.

PREPARATION TIME: 40 MINUTES   COOKING TIME: 12 MINUTES

BANANA CAKE

125 g (4$^{1}/_{2}$ oz) unsalted butter, softened
115 g (4 oz/$^{1}/_{2}$ cup) caster (superfine) sugar
2 eggs, lightly beaten
1 teaspoon natural vanilla extract
4 very ripe bananas, mashed
1 teaspoon bicarbonate of soda (baking soda)
125 ml (4 fl oz/$^{1}/_{2}$ cup) milk
250 g (9 oz/2 cups) self-raising flour, sifted
$^{1}/_{2}$ teaspoon ground mixed (pumpkin pie) spice
15 g ($^{1}/_{2}$ oz/$^{1}/_{4}$ cup) flaked coconut, toasted

BUTTER FROSTING
125 g (4$^{1}/_{2}$ oz) unsalted butter, softened
90 g (3$^{1}/_{4}$ oz/$^{3}/_{4}$ cup) icing (confectioners') sugar
1 tablespoon lemon juice

SERVES 8

Preheat the oven to 180°C (350°F/Gas 4). Lightly grease a 20 cm (8 inch) round cake tin and line the base with baking paper. Cream the butter and sugar in a small bowl using electric beaters until light and creamy. Add the egg gradually, beating thoroughly after each addition. Add the vanilla and banana and beat until combined. Transfer to a large bowl.

Dissolve the bicarbonate of soda in the milk. Using a metal spoon, gently fold the sifted flour and mixed spice alternately with the milk into the banana mixture. Stir until all the ingredients are just combined and the mixture is smooth. Spoon into the prepared tin and smooth the surface. Bake for 1 hour, or until a skewer inserted into the centre of the cake comes out clean. Leave the cake in the tin for 10 minutes before turning out onto a wire rack to cool completely.

To make the frosting, beat the butter, icing sugar and lemon juice using electric beaters until smooth and creamy. Spread over the cooled cake using a flat-bladed knife and sprinkle with the toasted coconut flakes.

PREPARATION TIME: 20 MINUTES   COOKING TIME: 1 HOUR

LEMON COCONUT CAKE

185 g (6$^{1}/_{2}$ oz/1$^{1}/_{2}$ cups) self-raising flour
45 g (1$^{3}/_{4}$ oz/$^{1}/_{2}$ cup) desiccated coconut
1 tablespoon grated lemon zest
230 g (8$^{1}/_{2}$ oz/1 cup) caster (superfine) sugar
125 g (4$^{1}/_{2}$ oz) unsalted butter, melted
2 eggs
250 ml (9 fl oz/1 cup) milk

COCONUT ICING
185 g (6$^{1}/_{2}$ oz/1$^{1}/_{2}$ cups) icing (confectioners') sugar, sifted
90 g (3$^{1}/_{4}$ oz/1 cup) desiccated coconut
$^{1}/_{2}$ teaspoon grated lemon zest
60 ml (2 fl oz/$^{1}/_{4}$ cup) lemon juice

SERVES 8

Preheat the oven to 180°C (350°F/Gas 4). Lightly grease a deep 20 cm (8 inch) round cake tin and line with baking paper.

Sift the flour into a large bowl and add the coconut, lemon zest, sugar, butter, eggs and milk. Mix well with a wooden spoon until smooth. Pour into the tin and smooth the surface. Bake for 40 minutes, or until a skewer inserted into the centre of the cake comes out clean. Leave the cake in the tin for 5 minutes before turning out onto a wire rack to cool completely.

To make the icing (frosting), combine the icing sugar and coconut in a bowl, then add the lemon zest and enough lemon juice to make a stiff but spreadable icing. Spread the icing over the cold cake.

PREPARATION TIME: 20 MINUTES +   COOKING TIME: 40 MINUTES

Banana cake

BLUEBERRY CHEESECAKE

125 g (4¹/2 oz) unsalted butter
100 g (3¹/2 oz/1 cup) rolled (porridge) oats
100 g (3¹/2 oz) wheatmeal biscuits, finely crushed
2 tablespoons soft brown sugar

FILLING
375 g (13 oz) light cream cheese
100 g (3¹/2 oz) ricotta cheese
80 g (2³/4 oz/¹/3 cup) caster (superfine) sugar
125 g (4¹/2 oz/¹/2 cup) sour cream
2 eggs
1 tablespoon finely grated orange zest
1 tablespoon plain (all-purpose) flour

TOPPING
250 g (9 oz) fresh blueberries
240 g (8³/4 oz/³/4 cup) spreadable blackberry fruit
60 ml (2 fl oz/¹/4 cup) cherry brandy

SERVES 8–10

Brush a 20 cm (8 inch) round deep spring-form cake tin with melted butter or oil and line the base with baking paper. Melt the butter in a saucepan, add the oats and biscuit crumbs and mix well. Stir in the sugar. Press half the biscuit mixture into the base of the tin and gradually press the remainder around the sides, using a glass to firm it into place, but not all the way up to the rim. Refrigerate for 10-15 minutes. Preheat the oven to 180°C (350°F/Gas 4).

To make the filling, beat the cream cheese, ricotta, sugar and sour cream in a bowl using electric beaters until smooth. Beat in the eggs, orange zest and flour until smooth. Put the tin on a baking tray to catch any drips, pour the filling into the crust and bake for 40-45 minutes, or until the filling is just set. Remove from the oven but leave in the tin to cool.

To make the topping, scatter the blueberries on top of the cheesecake. Sieve the spreadable fruit into a small saucepan with the brandy. Stir over medium heat until smooth and then simmer for 2-3 minutes. Carefully brush over the blueberries. Refrigerate for several hours or overnight.

PREPARATION TIME: 40 MINUTES +   COOKING TIME: 50 MINUTES

LEMON CAKE WITH CRUNCHY TOPPING

250 g (9 oz) unsalted butter, softened
200 g (7 oz) caster (superfine) sugar
2 teaspoons finely grated lemon zest
4 eggs, lightly beaten
250 g (9 oz/2 cups) self-raising flour
1 teaspoon baking powder
2 tablespoons lemon juice

CRUNCHY TOPPING
110 g ($3^3/4$ oz/$^1/2$ cup) sugar
60 ml (2 fl oz/$^1/4$ cup) lemon juice

SERVES 8–10

Preheat the oven to 170°C (325°F/Gas 3). Lightly grease a 22 cm ($8^1/2$ inch) square cake tin and line the base with baking paper. Cream the butter and sugar in a small bowl using electric beaters until the mixture is light and fluffy. Beat in the lemon zest, then gradually add the egg, beating thoroughly after each addition. Transfer the mixture to a large bowl. Using a large metal spoon, fold in the combined sifted flour, baking powder and $^1/4$ teaspoon salt, as well as the lemon juice. Stir until the mixture is just combined and almost smooth. Spoon the mixture into the tin and smooth the surface. Bake for 1 hour 20 minutes, or until a skewer inserted into the centre of the cake comes out clean. Remove from the tin and turn out onto a wire rack. To make the topping, mix together the sugar and lemon juice (do not dissolve the sugar), and quickly brush over the top of the warm cake. The juice will sink into the cake, and the sugar will form a crunchy topping. Cool.

PREPARATION TIME: 25 MINUTES   COOKING TIME: 1 HOUR 20 MINUTES

CHOCOLATE SWISS ROLL

3 eggs
115 g (4 oz/$^1/2$ cup) caster (superfine) sugar
30 g (1 oz/$^1/4$ cup) plain (all-purpose) flour
2 tablespoons unsweetened cocoa powder
250 ml (9 fl oz/1 cup) pouring (whipping) cream
1 tablespoon icing (confectioners') sugar
$^1/2$ teaspoon natural vanilla extract
icing (confectioners') sugar, extra, to dust

SERVES 10–12

Preheat the oven to 200°C (400°F/Gas 6). Lightly grease the base and sides of a 2 x 25 x 30 cm ($^3/4$ x 10 x 12 inch) Swiss roll tin (jelly roll tin). Line the base with baking paper, extending over the two long sides. Beat the eggs and 80 g ($2^3/4$ oz/$^1/3$ cup) of the caster sugar in a small bowl until thick and creamy. Using a metal spoon, gently fold in the combined sifted flour and cocoa powder. Spread the mixture into the tin and smooth the surface. Bake for about 10–12 minutes, or until the cake is just set. Meanwhile, place a clean tea towel (dish towel) on a work surface, cover with baking paper and sprinkle with the remaining caster sugar. As soon as the cake is cooked, turn it out onto the sugar. Roll the cake up from the short side, rolling the paper inside the roll and using the tea towel as a guide. Stand the rolled cake on a wire rack for 5 minutes, then carefully unroll and allow the cake to cool to room temperature. Trim the ends with a knife.

Beat the cream, icing sugar and vanilla until stiff peaks form. Spread the cream over the cooled cake, leaving a 1 cm ($^1/2$ inch) border all around. Re-roll the cake, using the paper as a guide. Place the roll, seam side down, on a tray. Refrigerate, covered, for 30 minutes. Lightly dust the top of the Swiss roll with icing sugar before cutting into slices to serve.

PREPARATION TIME: 25 MINUTES +   COOKING TIME: 12 MINUTES

STRAWBERRIES AND CREAM SPONGE WITH SPUN TOFFEE

75 g (2³/4 oz) plain (all-purpose) flour
150 g (5¹/2 oz) self-raising flour
6 eggs
220 g (7³/4 oz) caster (superfine) sugar
2 tablespoons boiling water
750 ml (26 fl oz/3 cups) pouring (whipping) cream
2 tablespoons icing (confectioners') sugar
500 g (1 lb 2 oz/3¹/3 cups) strawberries
Kirsch or Cointreau, to brush
230 g (8¹/2 oz/1 cup) caster (superfine) sugar, extra

SERVES 10–12

Preheat the oven to 180°C (350°F/Gas 4). Grease two deep 22 cm (8¹/2 inch) round cake tins and line the bases with baking paper. Lightly dust the tins with flour, shaking off the excess. Sift the flours three times onto baking paper. Beat the eggs in a large bowl using electric beaters for 7 minutes, or until thick and pale.

Add the sugar gradually to the eggs, beating thoroughly after each addition. Using a metal spoon, fold in the sifted flour and boiling water. Spread the mixture evenly into the tins and bake for 25 minutes, or until the sponges are lightly golden and shrink slightly from the sides of the tins. Leave the sponges in their tins for 5 minutes before turning out onto a wire rack to cool.

Using a serrated knife, slice each cake horizontally in half (you will only need three layers of cake, so freeze the remaining portion for trifles or cake crumbs). Whip the cream and icing sugar into stiff peaks. Hull the strawberries and thinly slice half of them.

Place one layer of cake on a serving plate or board and brush lightly with a little liqueur. Spread with one-quarter of the cream and scatter with half the sliced strawberries. Repeat with another layer of cake, liqueur, cream and sliced strawberries. Place the last cake layer on top and spread the remaining cream roughly over the top. Arrange the remaining whole strawberries on top. Refrigerate until the toffee is ready.

To make the toffee, put a heavy-based frying pan over medium heat, gradually sprinkle with some of the extra sugar and, as it melts, sprinkle with the remaining sugar. Stir to melt any lumps and prevent the sugar burning. When the toffee is golden brown, remove the pan immediately from the heat.

Dip two forks in the toffee, then rub the backs of the forks together until the toffee begins to stick. Gently pull the forks apart to check whether the toffee is cool enough to spin. If it drips or dips, it probably needs a little longer to cool. If not, continue pulling the toffee apart over the cake, pressing the forks together to spin a second time when they meet. Re-dip and continue spinning backwards and forwards and over the cake. Serve as soon as you've spun the toffee.

PREPARATION TIME: 40 MINUTES +   COOKING TIME: 30 MINUTES

CHOCOLATE COLLAR CHEESECAKE

200 g (7 oz) plain chocolate biscuits (cookies), crushed

70 g (2^1/$_2$ oz) unsalted butter, melted

500 g (1 lb 2 oz/2 cups) cream cheese, softened

75 g (2^3/$_4$ oz/^{1}/$_3$ cup) sugar

2 eggs

1 tablespoon unsweetened cocoa powder

300 g (10^1/$_2$ oz) sour cream

250 g (9 oz) dark chocolate, melted

80 ml (2^1/$_2$ fl oz/^{1}/$_3$ cup) Bailey's Irish Cream

50 g (1^3/$_4$ oz) white chocolate, melted

150 g (5^1/$_2$ oz) dark chocolate, melted

310 ml (10^3/$_4$ fl oz/1^1/$_4$ cups) whipped cream

unsweetened cocoa powder and icing (confectioners') sugar, to dust

SERVES 8–10

Brush a 23 cm (9 inch) round spring-form cake tin with melted butter and line the base and side with baking paper. Mix together the biscuit crumbs and butter, press firmly into the base of the tin and refrigerate for 10 minutes. Preheat the oven to 180°C (350°F/Gas 4). Beat the cream cheese and sugar using electric beaters until smooth and creamy. Add the eggs, one at a time, beating thoroughly after each addition. Beat in the cocoa and sour cream until smooth. Beat in the cooled melted dark chocolate. Beat in the liqueur and pour over the base. Smooth the surface and bake for 45 minutes. The cheesecake may not be fully set, but will firm up. Refrigerate, until cold.

Remove the cheesecake from the tin and put it on a board. Measure the height and add 5 mm (^{1}/$_4$ inch). Cut a strip of baking paper this wide and 75 cm (29^1/$_2$ inches) long. Pipe or drizzle the melted white chocolate in a figure eight pattern along the paper. When just set, spread the dark chocolate over the entire strip of paper. Allow the chocolate to set a little, but you need to be able to bend the paper without it cracking. Wrap the paper around the cheesecake with the chocolate inside. Seal the ends and hold the paper in place until the chocolate is completely set. Peel away the paper. Spread the top with cream, then dust with cocoa and icing sugar.

PREPARATION TIME: 1 HOUR 30 MINUTES + COOKING TIME: 50 MINUTES

MINI CHEESECAKES

250 g (9 oz) sweet biscuits (cookies)

125 g (4^1/$_2$ oz) unsalted butter, melted

3 teaspoons powdered gelatine

60 ml (2 fl oz/^{1}/$_4$ cup) boiling water

250 g (9 oz/1 cup) cream cheese, softened

80 g (2^3/$_4$ oz/^{1}/$_3$ cup) caster (superfine) sugar

150 g (5^1/$_2$ oz) chocolate, melted

2 teaspoons grated orange zest

60 ml (2 fl oz/^{1}/$_4$ cup) Tia Maria

300 ml (10^1/$_2$ fl oz) pouring (whipping) cream

MAKES 48

Grease four deep 12-hole patty pans or mini muffin tins and place a thin strip of baking paper in the bases, extending up the sides. Finely crush the biscuits. Stir in the butter, then firmly press 1 heaped teaspoon into each patty pan base. Refrigerate.

Dissolve the gelatine in the boiling water. Beat the cream cheese with the sugar, then add the melted chocolate, orange zest and Tia Maria, and beat until smooth. Stir in the gelatine, spoon onto the bases and refrigerate for 2 hours, or until firm. Whip the cream and spoon over the cheesecakes. Garnish with chocolate curls, if desired.

PREPARATION TIME: 30 MINUTES + COOKING TIME: 5 MINUTES

Chocolate collar cheesecake

MERINGUE AND BERRY CAKE

COCONUT CAKE

500 g (1 lb 2 oz/4 cups) self-raising flour

90 g (3¼ oz/1 cup) desiccated coconut

440 g (15½ oz) caster (superfine) sugar

135 g (4¾ oz/1⅓ cups) ground almonds

500 ml (17 fl oz/2 cups) buttermilk

4 eggs

2 teaspoons natural vanilla extract

300 g (10½ oz) unsalted butter, melted

110 g (3¾ oz) caster (superfine) sugar

60 ml (2 fl oz/¼ cup) Cointreau or orange juice

750 g (1 lb 10 oz) assorted fresh berries (such as blueberries, raspberries, blackberries or loganberries)

icing (confectioners') sugar, to dust (optional)

MERINGUE FROSTING

3 egg whites

165 g (5¾ oz) caster (superfine) sugar

250 g (9 oz) unsalted butter, softened

SERVES 8–10

Preheat the oven to 180°C (350°F/Gas 4). Lightly grease two deep 20 cm (8 inch) round cake tins and line the bases with baking paper.

Sift the flour into a large bowl and add the coconut, sugar and almonds. Mix well, then make a well in the centre. Pour the combined buttermilk, eggs, vanilla and butter into the well and stir with a metal spoon until smooth. If you don't have a bowl big enough, then make the mixture in two batches.

Pour the mixture into the tins and smooth the surface. Bake for 1¼ hours. If your oven is large enough, it is best to cook both cakes on the middle shelf, but make sure that the tins are not touching each other and that they are not touching the sides of the oven. Alternatively, the cakes can be baked on different shelves but they will need to be rotated after 50 minutes cooking time because the cake on the higher shelf may colour a little more than the other cake. Cover the cakes lightly with foil for the last 15 minutes, if necessary, so they don't burn. The cakes are ready when a skewer inserted into the centre of the cake comes out clean. Leave in the tin for 10 minutes before turning out onto a wire rack to cool.

To make the frosting, put the egg whites and sugar in a heatproof bowl. Bring a small saucepan of water to a simmer and place the bowl over the pan, making sure the base of the bowl does not touch the water. Stir to dissolve the sugar, but be careful not to cook the egg whites. When the sugar has dissolved, remove from the heat and beat using electric beaters for 5 minutes, or until stiff peaks form. Cut the butter into about 10 pieces and add, piece by piece, beating after each addition. The mixture should thicken when you have a couple of pieces of butter left, but continue until you have added it all.

Put the caster sugar in a small saucepan with 185 ml (6 fl oz/¾ cup) water and stir over the heat until the sugar has dissolved. Stir in the Cointreau.

Trim the domed top off each cake to give a flat surface. Slice each cake in half horizontally and place one layer on a serving plate or board. Brush well with the Cointreau syrup and spread with a thin layer of frosting. Repeat this to build up the layers, finishing with a layer of cake. Spread the remaining frosting evenly over the top and side of the cake with a palette or flat-bladed knife. Spread the frosting up the side of the cake to make furrows. Pile the berries on top of the cake. Dust with a little icing (confectioners') sugar if you prefer your berries sweetened.

PREPARATION TIME: 1 HOUR   COOKING TIME: 1 HOUR 30 MINUTES

SACHER TORTE

125 g (4¹/₂ oz/1 cup) plain (all-purpose) flour
30 g (1 oz/¹/₄ cup) unsweetened cocoa powder
230 g (8¹/₂ oz/1 cup) caster (superfine) sugar
100 g (3¹/₂ oz) unsalted butter
80 g (2³/₄ oz/¹/₄ cup) strawberry jam
4 eggs, separated

GANACHE TOPPING
170 ml (5¹/₂ fl oz/²/₃ cup) pouring (whipping) cream
80 g (2³/₄ oz/¹/₃ cup) caster (superfine) sugar
200 g (7 oz) dark chocolate, chopped

SERVES 10–12

Preheat the oven to 180°C (350°F/Gas 4). Lightly grease a 20 cm (8 inch) round cake tin and line with baking paper. Sift the flour and cocoa into a large bowl and make a well in the centre. Combine the sugar, butter and half the jam in a small saucepan. Stir over low heat until the butter has melted and the sugar has dissolved, then add to the flour with the lightly beaten egg yolks and stir until just combined.

Beat the egg whites in a small, dry, clean bowl using electric beaters until soft peaks form. Stir one-third of the egg white into the cake mixture, then fold in the rest in two batches. Pour into the tin and smooth the surface. Bake for 40–45 minutes, or until a skewer inserted into the centre comes out clean. Leave in the tin for 15 minutes before turning out onto a wire rack to cool.

To make the topping, stir the cream, sugar and chocolate in a small saucepan over low heat until melted and smooth. Trim the top of the cake so that it is flat, then turn it upside down on a wire rack over a tray. Melt the remaining jam and brush it over the cake. Pour most of the topping over the cake and tap the tray to flatten the surface. Place the remaining mixture in a piping (icing) bag and pipe 'Sacher' on the top of the cake.

PREPARATION TIME: 40 MINUTES +   COOKING TIME: 50 MINUTES

JAFFA TRIPLE-CHOC BROWNIES

125 g (4¹/₂ oz) unsalted butter, cubed
350 g (12 oz) dark chocolate, roughly chopped
185 g (6¹/₂ oz/1 cup) soft brown sugar
3 eggs
2 teaspoons grated orange zest
125 g (4¹/₂ oz/1 cup) plain (all-purpose) flour
30 g (1 oz/¹/₄ cup) unsweetened cocoa powder
100 g (3¹/₂ oz) milk chocolate chips
100 g (3¹/₂ oz) white chocolate chips

MAKES 25

Preheat the oven to 180°C (350°F/Gas 4). Lightly grease a 23 cm (9 inch) square shallow tin and line with baking paper, leaving the paper hanging over on two opposite sides. Place the butter and 250 g (9 oz) of the dark chocolate in a heatproof bowl. Half-fill a saucepan with water, bring to the boil, then remove from the heat. Sit the bowl over the saucepan, making sure the base of the bowl does not touch the water. Stir occasionally until the butter and chocolate have melted. Cool.

Beat the sugar, eggs and orange zest in a bowl until thick and fluffy. Fold in the chocolate mixture. Sift the flour and cocoa into a bowl, then stir into the chocolate mixture. Stir in the remaining dark chocolate and all the chocolate chips. Spread into the tin and bake for 40 minutes, or until just cooked. Cool in the tin before lifting out, using the paper as handles, and cutting into squares. Can be drizzled with melted dark chocolate.

PREPARATION TIME: 20 MINUTES   COOKING TIME: 45 MINUTES

ORANGE AND LEMON SYRUP CAKE

BUTTER CAKE
185 g (6^1/$_2$ oz/1^1/$_2$ cups) self-raising flour
60 g (2^1/$_4$ oz/^{1}/$_2$ cup) plain (all-purpose) flour
185 g (6^1/$_2$ oz) unsalted butter, chopped and softened
170 g (6 oz/^{3}/$_4$ cup) caster (superfine) sugar
3 eggs, lightly beaten
1 teaspoon natural vanilla extract
1 teaspoon grated orange zest
60 ml (2 fl oz/^{1}/$_4$ cup) milk

SYRUP
2 oranges
2 lemons
520 g (1 lb 2^1/$_2$ oz) caster (superfine) sugar

SERVES 10–12

Preheat the oven to 180°C (350°F/Gas 4). Lightly grease a 20 cm (8 inch) kugelhopf tin. Dust lightly with flour.

Sift the flours into a bowl. Cream the butter and sugar in a small bowl using electric beaters until light and fluffy. With the beaters still running, add the egg gradually, a little at a time, beating thoroughly after each addition. Add the vanilla and beat well to combine. Transfer the mixture to a large bowl and, using a large metal spoon, gently fold in the sifted flour, orange zest and milk. Stir until just combined and almost smooth. Spoon the mixture into the tin and cook for 1 hour 5 minutes, or until a skewer inserted into the centre of the cake comes out clean.

Cut the oranges and lemons into thin slices, without peeling them. To make the syrup, place 250 g (9 oz) of the sugar in a heavy-based frying pan with 80 ml (2^1/$_2$ fl oz/^{1}/$_3$ cup) water. Stir over low heat until the sugar has completely dissolved. Bring to the boil, then reduce the heat and simmer. Add a quarter of the sliced fruit to the syrup and leave to simmer for 5–10 minutes, or until transparent and toffee-like. Lift out the fruit with tongs and cool on a wire rack. Add an extra 90 g (3^1/$_4$ oz) of sugar to the syrup and stir gently to dissolve — the juice from the fruit breaks down the concentrated syrup and the fruit won't candy properly unless you add the sugar. Simmer the second batch of sliced fruit. Add 90 g (3^1/$_4$ oz) of sugar to the syrup before cooking each batch.

When all the fruit has been candied, turn the cake out onto a wire rack over a tray and pour the hot syrup over the warm cake, allowing it to soak in — if the syrup is too thick, thin it with a little orange juice. Put the cake on a serving plate. When the fruit slices have firmed, arrange them on top of the cake (you can cut and twist some of the slices).

PREPARATION TIME: 40 MINUTES   COOKING TIME: 1 HOUR 50 MINUTES

NOTES: The candied fruit can be kept between layers of baking paper in an airtight container for up to 2 days.

The cake should be served within a few hours of decorating. If you prefer, you can bake this cake in a 20 cm (8 inch) round tin.

CHOCOLATE MUD CAKE

250 g (9 oz) unsalted butter

250 g (9 oz) dark chocolate, broken

2 tablespoons instant coffee powder

150 g (5½ oz) self-raising flour

155 g (5½ oz/1¼ cups) plain (all-purpose) flour

60 g (2¼ oz/½ cup) unsweetened cocoa powder

½ teaspoon bicarbonate of soda (baking soda)

550 g (1 lb 4 oz/2½ cups) sugar

4 eggs

2 tablespoons oil

125 ml (4 fl oz/½ cup) buttermilk

chocolate, extra, to decorate

GLAZE

250 g (9 oz) dark chocolate, chopped

125 ml (4 fl oz/½ cup) pouring (whipping) cream

145 g (5½ oz/⅔ cup) caster (superfine) sugar

SERVES 8–10

Preheat the oven to 160°C (315°F/Gas 2–3). Brush a deep 22 cm (8½ inch) round cake tin with melted butter or oil. Line the base and side with baking paper, extending at least 2 cm (¾ inch) above the rim. Stir the butter, chocolate, coffee and 185 ml (6 fl oz/¾ cup) hot water in a saucepan, over low heat, until melted and smooth. Remove from the heat.

Sift the flours, cocoa and bicarbonate of soda into a large bowl. Stir in the sugar and make a well in the centre. Add the combined eggs, oil and buttermilk and, using a large metal spoon, slowly stir in the dry ingredients, then the melted chocolate mixture until combined. Spoon the mixture into the tin and bake for 1 hour 40 minutes, or until a skewer inserted into the centre of the cake comes out clean. Cool in the tin. When completely cold, remove from the tin.

To make the glaze, stir all the ingredients in a saucepan over low heat until melted. Bring to the boil, reduce the heat and simmer for 4–5 minutes. Remove from the heat and cool slightly. Put a wire rack on a baking tray and transfer the cake to the rack. Pour the glaze over the cake, making sure the sides are evenly covered. Decorate with chocolate.

PREPARATION TIME: 30 MINUTES +   COOKING TIME: 1 HOUR 55 MINUTES

ORANGE AND ALMOND CAKE

2 large oranges, skins scrubbed with warm water to remove wax coating

5 eggs

250 g (9 oz) ground almonds

220 g (7¾ oz/1 cup) sugar

1 teaspoon baking powder

icing (confectioners') sugar, to dust

SERVES 8–10

Lightly grease a 22 cm (8½ inch) spring-form cake tin and line the base with baking paper. Put the whole oranges in a saucepan, cover with water and boil for 1 hour. Remove from the water and set aside to cool. Preheat the oven to 180°C (350°F/Gas 4). Using a plate to catch any juice, cut the cooled oranges into quarters and remove any seeds. Blend the orange quarters, including the skin, in a food processor until they turn to a pulp.

Beat the eggs in a large bowl using electric beaters until light and fluffy. Add the orange pulp and any reserved juice, almonds, sugar and baking powder, mix thoroughly, then pour into the tin. Bake for 1 hour, or until the cake is firm to the touch and lightly golden. Cool in the tin before turning out onto a wire rack. Dust with sifted icing sugar before serving.

PREPARATION TIME: 20 MINUTES +   COOKING TIME: 2 HOURS

Chocolate mud cake

GINGER CAKE

125 g (4½ oz) unsalted butter
175 g (6 oz/½ cup) black treacle or molasses
175 g (6 oz/½ cup) golden syrup or dark corn syrup
185 g (6½ oz/1½ cups) plain (all-purpose) flour
125 g (4½ oz/1 cup) self-raising flour
1 teaspoon bicarbonate of soda (baking soda)
3 teaspoons ground ginger
1 teaspoon ground mixed (pumpkin pie) spice
¼ teaspoon ground cinnamon
165 g (5¾ oz/¾ cup) firmly packed soft brown sugar
250 ml (9 fl oz/1 cup) milk
2 eggs, lightly beaten
glacé ginger, to decorate (optional)

LEMON AND GINGER ICING
250 g (9 oz/2 cups) icing (confectioners') sugar
1 teaspoon ground ginger
30 g (1 oz) unsalted butter, melted
3 teaspoons milk
3 teaspoons lemon juice
1 teaspoon lemon zest

SERVES 8–10

Preheat the oven to 180°C (350°F/Gas 4). Lightly grease a deep 20 cm (8 inch) square cake tin and line the base with baking paper.

Combine the butter, treacle and golden syrup in a saucepan and stir over low heat until the butter has melted. Remove from the heat.

Sift the flours, bicarbonate of soda and spices into a large bowl, add the sugar and stir until well combined. Make a well in the centre. Add the butter mixture to the well, then pour in the combined milk and egg. Stir with a wooden spoon until the mixture is smooth and well combined. Pour into the tin and smooth the surface. Bake for 45–60 minutes, or until a skewer inserted into the centre of the cake comes out clean. Leave in the tin for 20 minutes before turning out onto a wire rack to cool.

To make the icing (frosting), sift the icing sugar into a small heatproof bowl and stir in the ground ginger, butter, milk, lemon juice and zest until the mixture forms a smooth paste. Stand the bowl over a saucepan of simmering water, making sure the base of the bowl does not touch the water. Stir until smooth and glossy, then remove from the heat. Spread over the cake with a flat-bladed knife. Decorate the top with glacé ginger, if desired.

PREPARATION TIME: 30 MINUTES +   COOKING TIME: 1 HOUR 5 MINUTES

NOTE: This delicious ginger cake can be served the day it is baked but it is best served 2 or 3 days after baking so the flavours have time to develop. It will store well for up to a week in an airtight container, or can be frozen, un-iced, for up to 3 months. It can also be served un-iced and decorated by lightly dusting the top with sifted icing sugar.

SAVOURY BITES

CHICKEN TAMALES

DOUGH
100 g (3¹/₂ oz) butter, softened
1 garlic clove, crushed
1 teaspoon ground cumin
210 g (7¹/₂ oz) masa harina (see NOTES)
80 ml (2¹/₂ fl oz/¹/₃ cup) pouring
(whipping) cream
80 ml (2¹/₂ fl oz/¹/₃ cup) chicken stock

FILLING
2 tomatoes
1 red capsicum (pepper)
1 corn cob
2 tablespoons oil
150 g (5¹/₂ oz) boneless, skinless chicken
breast
2 garlic cloves, crushed
1 red chilli, seeded and chopped
1 red onion, chopped

oregano, to garnish
chives, to garnish

MAKES 12

To make the dough, beat the butter using electric beaters until creamy. Add the garlic, cumin and 1 teaspoon salt and mix well. Add the masa harina and combined cream and stock alternately, beating until combined.

To make the filling, score a cross in the base of each tomato. Put in a heatproof bowl and cover with boiling water. Leave for 30 seconds, then transfer to cold water, drain and peel away the skin from the cross. Cut the tomatoes in half, scoop out the seeds and chop the flesh.

Cut the capsicum in half, remove the seeds and membrane and chop. Put the corn in a saucepan of boiling water and cook for 5–8 minutes, or until tender. Cool, then cut off the kernels with a sharp knife. Heat the oil in a frying pan and cook the chicken until golden. Remove, cool and finely shred. Add the garlic, chilli and onion to the pan and cook until soft. Add the capsicum and corn and stir for 3 minutes. Add the chicken, tomato and 1 teaspoon salt and simmer for 15 minutes, or until the liquid has reduced.

Bring a large saucepan of water to the boil and place a large bamboo steamer over it, making sure it doesn't touch the water.

Cut 12 pieces of baking paper 15 x 20 cm (6 x 8 inches). Spread a thick layer of dough over each piece, leaving a border at each end. Place some filling in the centre, roll up and secure both ends with string. Cook in the steamer for 35 minutes, or until firm. Serve whole or sliced, garnished with oregano and chives.

PREPARATION TIME: 45 MINUTES   COOKING TIME: 1 HOUR 15 MINUTES

NOTES: The filling can be made a day ahead. Assemble the tamales on the day of serving.

Masa harina is a heavy type of white flour made from maize.

CHEESE SCONES

250 g (9 oz/2 cups) self-raising flour
1 teaspoon baking powder
1/2 teaspoon dry mustard
30 g (1 oz) butter, chilled and cubed
25 g (1 oz/1/4 cup) freshly grated parmesan cheese
90 g (3 1/4 oz/3/4 cup) finely grated cheddar cheese
250 ml (9 fl oz/1 cup) milk

MAKES 12

Preheat the oven to 220°C (425°F/Gas 7). Lightly grease a baking tray or line with baking paper. Sift the flour, baking powder, mustard and a pinch of salt into a bowl. Using your fingertips, rub in the butter until the mixture resembles fine breadcrumbs. Stir in the parmesan and 60 g (2 1/4 oz/1/2 cup) of the cheddar cheese, making sure they don't clump together. Make a well in the centre.

Add almost all the milk and mix with a flat-bladed knife, using a cutting action, until the dough comes together in clumps. Use the remaining milk if necessary. With floured hands, gently gather the dough together, lift out onto a lightly floured surface and pat into a smooth ball. Do not knead or the scones will be tough.

Pat the dough out to 2 cm (3/4 inch) thick. Using a floured 5 cm (2 inch) biscuit (cookie) cutter, cut into rounds. Gather the trimmings and, without over-handling, press out as before and cut more rounds. Place the rounds close together on the tray and sprinkle with the remaining cheese. Bake for 12–15 minutes, or until risen and golden brown. Serve warm or at room temperature.

PREPARATION TIME: 15 MINUTES   COOKING TIME: 15 MINUTES

ANCHOVY AND TOMATO CROSTINI

1 baguette
olive oil, for brushing
250 g (9 oz/1 cup) sun-dried tomato pesto
50 g (1 3/4 oz) thinly sliced anchovy fillets, drained
50 g (1 3/4 oz/1/3 cup) chopped black olives
basil, finely shredded, to sprinkle

MAKES ABOUT 15

Cut the baguette into thick diagonal slices. Brush lightly with olive oil and toast until golden.

Spread the toasted baguette slices with the pesto and sprinkle the anchovy fillets, olives and the basil over the top.

PREPARATION TIME: 10 MINUTES   COOKING TIME: 3 MINUTES

CHICKEN SAUSAGE ROLLS

3 sheets frozen puff pastry, thawed
2 eggs, lightly beaten
750 g (1 lb 10 oz) minced (ground) chicken
4 spring onions (scallions), finely chopped
80 g (2³/₄ oz/1 cup) fresh breadcrumbs
1 carrot, finely grated
2 tablespoons fruit chutney
1 tablespoon sweet chilli sauce
1 tablespoon grated fresh ginger
sesame seeds, to sprinkle

MAKES 36

Preheat the oven to 200°C (400°F/Gas 6). Lightly grease two baking trays.

Cut the pastry sheets in half and lightly brush the edges with some of the beaten egg.

Mix half the remaining egg with the remaining ingredients, except the sesame seeds, in a large bowl, then divide into six even portions. Pipe or spoon the filling down the centre of each piece of pastry, then brush the edges with some of the egg. Fold the pastry over the filling, overlapping the edges and placing the join underneath.

Brush the rolls with more egg, sprinkle with sesame seeds, then cut each into six short pieces.

Cut two small slashes on top of each roll, place on the baking trays and bake for 15 minutes. Reduce the heat to 180°C (350°F/Gas 4) and bake for another 15 minutes, or until puffed and golden.

PREPARATION TIME: 30 MINUTES   COOKING TIME: 30 MINUTES

GRAHAM CRACKERS

350 g (12 oz/2$\frac{1}{3}$ cups) wholemeal (whole-wheat) plain (all-purpose) flour
60 g (2$\frac{1}{4}$ oz/$\frac{1}{2}$ cup) cornflour (cornstarch)
55 g (2 oz/$\frac{1}{4}$ cup) caster (superfine) sugar
150 g (5$\frac{1}{2}$ oz) butter
185 ml (6 fl oz/$\frac{3}{4}$ cup) pouring (whipping) cream

MAKES 12

Sift the flours into a bowl, then stir in the sugar and $\frac{1}{2}$ teaspoon salt. Rub in the butter with your fingertips until the mixture resembles breadcrumbs. Mix in the cream with a flat-bladed knife, using a cutting action, to make a pliable dough.

Gather the dough together and shape into a disc. Wrap in plastic wrap and refrigerate for 30 minutes.

Preheat the oven to 200°C (400°F/Gas 6). Line two baking trays with baking paper.

Roll out the dough to a rectangle measuring 24 x 30 cm (9$\frac{1}{2}$ x 12 inches). Cut the dough into 12 rectangles with a sharp knife or pastry wheel. Place the rectangles on the baking trays, allowing a little room for spreading.

Bake for 7–10 minutes, or until firm and golden brown. Leave to cool on the trays for 2–3 minutes, before transferring to a wire rack to cool completely. When the crackers are cold, store in an airtight container.

PREPARATION TIME: 25 MINUTES +   COOKING TIME: 10 MINUTES

SOFT CHEESE PÂTÉ

155 g (5$\frac{1}{2}$ oz/1 cup) pine nuts, toasted
500 g (1 lb 2 oz/3$\frac{1}{3}$ cups) crumbled feta cheese
185 ml (6 fl oz/$\frac{3}{4}$ cup) pouring (whipping) cream
30 g (1 oz) chopped mint
30 g (1 oz) chopped dill
30 g (1 oz) chopped flat-leaf (Italian) parsley

SERVES 12–15

Roughly chop the pine nuts in a food processor. Add the feta cheese, cream and 2 teaspoons coarsely ground pepper and mix until smooth. Add the mint, dill and parsley and process until just combined.

Line a 750 ml (26 fl oz/3 cup) bowl with plastic wrap. Transfer the mixture to the bowl and press in firmly. Refrigerate, covered, for at least 1 hour, or until firm. Turn out onto a plate and smooth the surface with a knife. Serve with toast triangles.

PREPARATION TIME: 15 MINUTES +   COOKING TIME: NIL

SMOKED SALMON ROLLS

6 eggs
3 teaspoons cornflour (cornstarch)
125 g (4$\frac{1}{2}$ oz/$\frac{1}{2}$ cup) cream cheese
2 tablespoons chopped pickled ginger
2 tablespoons snipped chives
200 g (7 oz) sliced smoked salmon, chopped
flat-leaf (Italian) parsley sprigs, to garnish

MAKES 36

Beat one egg in a bowl with 1 teaspoon water and $\frac{1}{2}$ teaspoon of the cornflour and season. Heat a frying pan and brush it lightly with oil. Add the egg and cook over medium heat, drawing the outside edges of the mixture into the centre with a spatula, until the mixture is lightly set. Cool in the pan for 2 minutes, then carefully slide out onto a clean, flat surface with the uncooked side upwards. Set aside to cool. Repeat the process with the remaining eggs, beaten with water and cornflour, to make five more omelettes.

Place each omelette on a sheet of baking paper on a flat surface. Divide the cream cheese among the omelettes, spreading over each. Sprinkle with pickled ginger, chives and salmon, then season with black pepper. Roll each gently but firmly, using the paper to help pull the roll towards you. Chill, wrapped in plastic wrap, for at least 3 hours.

Using a sharp knife, cut the rolls into 2 cm ($\frac{3}{4}$ inch) slices, discarding the uneven ends. Garnish with parsley sprigs.

PREPARATION TIME: 30 MINUTES + COOKING TIME: 5 MINUTES

NOTE: These rolls can be made a day ahead, covered and refrigerated. Serve at room temperature.

CAPSICUM ROLLS

1 large red capsicum (pepper)
60 g (2¼ oz) cheddar cheese, grated
30 g (1 oz) parmesan cheese, freshly grated
2 tablespoons whole-egg mayonnaise
2 tablespoons finely chopped flat-leaf (Italian) parsley
1 teaspoon chopped thyme
1 teaspoon chopped oregano
2 drops Tabasco sauce
10 slices fresh bread
45 g (1¾ oz) butter, melted
paprika, to sprinkle

MAKES 20

Cut the red capsicum in half and remove the seeds and membrane. Cook, skin side up, under a hot grill (broiler) until the skin is black and blistered. Place in a plastic bag and leave to cool, then peel. Finely chop the flesh and combine in a bowl with the cheddar, parmesan, mayonnaise, herbs and Tabasco, then season. Cut the crusts from the bread, flatten the slices well with a rolling pin and brush both sides with the melted butter.

Spread the capsicum mixture on each slice, leaving a 1 cm (½ inch) border. Roll up and secure with toothpicks. Cover and refrigerate for at least 2 hours.

Preheat the oven to 180°C (350°F/Gas 4). Cut each roll in half and secure with a toothpick. Bake on a baking tray for about 10–12 minutes, or until the rolls are crisp and pale golden. Sprinkle with paprika. Serve warm.

PREPARATION TIME: 30 MINUTES +   COOKING TIME: 12 MINUTES

NOTE: These rolls can be prepared and refrigerated up to a day in advance and baked just before serving.

PAN-FRIED CHEESE SANDWICHES

20 thick slices white bread
2–3 tablespoons dijon mustard
10 slices cheddar cheese
oil, for pan-frying
plain (all-purpose) flour, for dusting
3 eggs, lightly beaten
watercress, trimmed, to garnish

MAKES 40

Remove the crusts from the bread. Spread the bread with mustard, place a slice of cheese on top, then finish with another bread slice. Heat a little oil in a frying pan. Dust the sandwiches lightly with flour and dip quickly into the beaten egg. Cook the sandwiches on both sides until golden, then drain on paper towels. Cut into quarters and garnish with watercress. Serve hot.

PREPARATION TIME: 20 MINUTES   COOKING TIME: 20 MINUTES

NOTE: Assemble the sandwiches up to 4 hours in advance, but don't dust with flour and dip in the egg until just before frying.

CHICKEN ROLLS

60 g (2¹/₄ oz) butter
1 large onion, chopped
2 garlic cloves, crushed
2 tablespoons plain (all-purpose) flour
125 ml (4 fl oz/¹/₂ cup) chicken stock
125 ml (4 fl oz/¹/₂ cup) milk
1 large barbecued chicken, skin removed and flesh shredded
25 g (1 oz/¹/₄ cup) freshly grated parmesan cheese
2 teaspoons thyme
25 g (1 oz/¹/₄ cup) dry breadcrumbs
2 eggs, lightly beaten
13 sheets filo pastry, cut into thirds crossways
140 g (5 oz) butter, extra, melted

MAKES ABOUT 40

Melt the butter in a saucepan and add the onion. Cook over low heat for 12 minutes, or until soft, stirring occasionally. Increase the heat to medium–high and add the garlic. Cook, stirring, for 1 minute, then add the flour and cook for 1 minute. Remove from the heat and gradually stir in the stock and milk. Return to the heat and stir constantly until the sauce boils and thickens. Boil for 1 minute, then remove from the heat and add the chicken, parmesan, thyme and breadcrumbs, then season. Cool, then stir in the egg.

Preheat the oven to 220°C (425°F/Gas 7). Lightly grease three baking trays. Put one piece of filo pastry on a flat surface with the short end closest to you — cover the remaining pieces with a damp tea towel (dish towel). Brush with the extra melted butter and place a level tablespoon of chicken mixture on the base end closest to you. Fold in the sides, brush along the length with butter and roll up tightly to form a roll 8 cm (3¹/₄ inches) long. Put onto the baking tray and brush the top with some of the butter. Repeat with the remaining filo, butter and chicken mixture.

Bake for 15 minutes in the top half of the oven until well browned. Serve hot.

PREPARATION TIME: 1 HOUR 15 MINUTES COOKING TIME: 35 MINUTES

INDIVIDUAL PUMPKIN AND CURRY QUICHES

CREAM CHEESE PASTRY
185 g (6$\frac{1}{2}$ oz/1$\frac{1}{2}$ cups) plain (all-purpose) flour
125 g (4$\frac{1}{2}$ oz/$\frac{1}{2}$ cup) cream cheese, chopped
125 g (4$\frac{1}{2}$ oz) butter, chopped

FILLING
1 tablespoon oil
2 onions, finely chopped
3 garlic cloves, crushed
1 teaspoon curry powder
3 eggs
125 ml (4 fl oz/$\frac{1}{2}$ cup) thick (double/heavy) cream
350 g (12 oz) pumpkin (winter squash), cooked and mashed
2 teaspoons cumin seeds

MAKES 8

Preheat the oven to 210°C (415°F/Gas 6–7). Grease eight deep 10 cm (4 inch) flan (tart) tins and line with baking paper.

To make the cream cheese pastry, sift the flour into a large bowl and add the cream cheese and butter. Using your fingertips, rub the ingredients together for 2 minutes, or until the mixture is smooth and comes together in a ball. Turn the dough onto a lightly floured surface, knead for 10 seconds, or until smooth. Cover with plastic wrap and refrigerate for 30 minutes. Divide the pastry into eight equal portions, roll out and line the tins. Bake for 15 minutes, or until lightly browned. Remove from the oven. Reduce the heat to 180°C (350°F/Gas 4).

To make the filling, heat the oil in a small frying pan, add the onion and garlic and stir over low heat for 5 minutes or until soft. Add the curry powder and stir for 1 minute. Spread over the bases of the pastry cases.

Combine the eggs, cream and pumpkin in a large bowl and beat until combined. Pour over the onion mixture, then sprinkle with the cumin seeds. Bake in the oven for 20 minutes, or until the filling has set.

PREPARATION TIME: 30 MINUTES +   COOKING TIME: 40 MINUTES

CURRIED APPLE AND ONION MINI QUICHES

2 sheets ready-rolled shortcrust (pie) pastry
oil, for pan-frying
1 small onion, thinly sliced
1 small apple, peeled and grated
$\frac{1}{4}$ teaspoon curry powder
125 ml (4 fl oz/$\frac{1}{2}$ cup) milk
2 eggs, lightly beaten
2 tablespoons pouring (whipping) cream
20 g ($\frac{3}{4}$ oz) grated cheddar cheese

MAKES 24

Preheat the oven to 200°C (400°F/Gas 6). Grease two round-based shallow 12-hole patty pans or mini muffin tins. Lay the shortcrust pastry on a work surface and cut 12 rounds from each sheet with an 8 cm (3$\frac{1}{4}$ inch) biscuit (cookie) cutter. Line the patty pans with pastry.

Heat a little oil in a frying pan. Lightly brown the onion, then add the apple. Add the curry powder and stir for 1 minute. Cool slightly. Spoon heaped teaspoons into the pastry cases. Mix the milk, egg and cream and pour enough into each pastry case to cover the onion and apple mixture. Sprinkle with the cheese. Bake for 15–20 minutes, or until puffed and golden. Remove from the patty pans while warm and transfer to wire racks to cool.

PREPARATION TIME: 20 MINUTES   COOKING TIME: 25 MINUTES

Individual pumpkin and curry quiches

ROAST CAPSICUM RICE TARTS

1 litre (35 fl oz/4 cups) vegetable stock
20 g (³/₄ oz) butter
95 g (3¹/₂ oz/¹/₂ cup) wild rice
140 g (5 oz/²/₃ cup) short-grain brown rice
1 egg, lightly beaten with 1 egg yolk
50 g (1³/₄ oz/¹/₂ cup) freshly grated parmesan cheese
2 green capsicums (peppers)
2 red capsicums (peppers)
2 yellow capsicums (peppers)
150 g (5¹/₂ oz) camembert cheese, thinly sliced
2 tablespoons oregano

MAKES 6

Grease six 10 cm (4 inch) loose-based fluted flan (tart) tins. Pour the stock into a saucepan and bring to the boil. Reduce the heat, cover and keep at a low simmer.

Melt the butter in a large saucepan over low heat, then stir in the rice until well coated. Add 125 ml (4 fl oz/¹/₂ cup) of the hot stock to the rice, stirring well. Increase the heat to medium and add the remaining stock, 250 ml (9 fl oz/1 cup) at a time, stirring, until it has been absorbed. This will take about 30 minutes. Remove from the heat and cool. Add the egg and parmesan and season to taste.

Divide the rice mixture among the prepared flan tins and press it around the base and sides. Allow to cool completely. Preheat the oven to 200°C (400°F/Gas 6).

Cut the capsicums in half and remove the seeds and membrane, then cut into large, flattish pieces. Grill (broil) or hold over a gas flame until the skin blackens and blisters. Put on a cutting board, cover with a tea towel (dish towel) and allow to cool. Peel off the skin and cut the flesh into smaller pieces.

Put the camembert slices in the bottom of the rice-lined tins and divide the capsicum evenly among the tarts. Bake for 30 minutes. Sprinkle the oregano over the top and serve hot.

PREPARATION TIME: 45 MINUTES +   COOKING TIME: 1 HOUR 5 MINUTES

SPICY VEGETABLE MUFFINS

250 g (9 oz/2 cups) self-raising flour
3 teaspoons curry powder
80 g (2³/₄ oz/¹/₂ cup) grated carrot
60 g (2¹/₄ oz/¹/₂ cup) grated orange sweet potato
125 g (4¹/₂ oz/1 cup) grated cheddar cheese
90 g (3¹/₄ oz) butter, melted
1 egg, lightly beaten
185 ml (6 fl oz/³/₄ cup) milk

MAKES 12

Preheat the oven to 180°C (350°F/Gas 4). Lightly grease a 12-hole standard muffin tin, or line the muffin tin with paper cases. Sift the flour, curry powder and some salt and pepper into a bowl. Add the carrot, sweet potato and cheese and mix through with your fingertips until the ingredients are evenly combined. Make a well in the centre.

Combine the butter, egg and milk and add to the flour mixture all at once. Using a wooden spoon, stir until the ingredients are just combined. Do not overmix — the batter will still be slightly lumpy.

Divide the mixture evenly among the holes — fill each hole to about three-quarters full. Bake for 20–25 minutes, or until golden and a skewer inserted into the centre of a muffin comes out clean. Leave in the tin for a couple of minutes. Gently loosen each muffin with a flat-bladed knife before turning out onto a wire rack. Serve warm or at room temperature

PREPARATION TIME: 20 MINUTES   COOKING TIME: 25 MINUTES

SPICY LAMB SAUSAGE ROLLS

3 sheets frozen puff pastry, thawed
2 eggs, lightly beaten
750 g (1 lb 10 oz) minced (ground) lamb
1 small onion, grated
80 g (2³/₄ oz/1 cup) fresh breadcrumbs
1 tablespoon soy sauce
2 teaspoons grated fresh ginger
2 teaspoons soft brown sugar
1 teaspoon ground coriander
¹/₂ teaspoon ground cumin
¹/₂ teaspoon sambal oelek
poppy seeds, to sprinkle

MAKES 36

Preheat the oven to 200°C (400°F/Gas 6). Cut the pastry sheets in half and lightly brush the edges with some of the beaten egg.

Mix half the remaining egg with the remaining ingredients, except the poppy seeds, in a large bowl, then divide into six even portions. Pipe or spoon the filling down the centre of each piece of pastry, then brush the edges with some of the egg. Fold the pastry over the filling, overlapping the edges and placing the join underneath. Brush the rolls with more egg, sprinkle with the poppy seeds, then cut each into six short pieces.

Cut two small slashes on top of each roll and place on lightly greased baking trays and bake for 15 minutes, then reduce the heat to 180°C (350°F/Gas 4) and bake for another 15 minutes, or until puffed and golden.

PREPARATION TIME: 30 MINUTES   COOKING TIME: 30 MINUTES

SMOKED SALMON PÂTÉ WITH CHIVE PIKELETS

125 g (4½ oz) smoked salmon
2 teaspoons softened butter
1 small onion, chopped
1½ teaspoons horseradish cream
30 g (1 oz) softened butter, extra
3 teaspoons chopped tarragon
1 lime, cut into tiny wedges
red or black caviar, to garnish

CHIVE PIKELETS
60 g (2¼ oz/½ cup) self-raising flour
1 tablespoon snipped chives
1 egg yolk, lightly beaten
125 ml (4 fl oz/½ cup) milk

MAKES ABOUT 30

Roughly chop the salmon. Heat the butter in a small saucepan, add the onion and cook until soft. Put the smoked salmon, onion, horseradish cream and extra butter in a food processor. Season and mix until smooth. Add the tarragon and process until the pâté is just combined.

To make the pikelets, sift the flour and a pinch of salt into a bowl. Stir in the chives and make a well in the centre. Gradually whisk in the egg yolk and enough milk to form a smooth lump-free batter, the consistency of thick cream. Set aside for 15 minutes, then lightly grease a non-stick frying pan and drop teaspoons of the batter into the pan. When bubbles appear on the surface of the pikelets, turn them over and brown the other side. Transfer to a wire rack to cool. Repeat with the remaining batter.

Pipe or spread the pâté onto the pikelets, garnish with a slice of lime and some caviar.

PREPARATION TIME: 30 MINUTES +   COOKING TIME: 40 MINUTES

NOTE: The pikelets may be assembled up to 3 hours ahead, covered and refrigerated.

CRAB AND SPRING ONION MINI QUICHES

6 sheets filo pastry
30 g (1 oz) butter, melted
4 spring onions (scallions), chopped and squeezed dry
340 g (11¾ oz) tinned crabmeat, drained
2 eggs
185 ml (6 fl oz/¾ cup) pouring (whipping) cream
1 tablespoon plain (all-purpose) flour
90 g (3¼ oz) gruyère or cheddar cheese, grated
thyme sprigs

MAKES 15

Preheat the oven to 180°C (350°F/Gas 4). Layer the filo pastry together with the melted butter. Cut 15 rounds with an 8 cm (3¼ inch) plain cutter and place in round-based patty pans or mini muffin tins.

Melt a little extra butter in a small frying pan and cook the spring onion until softened. Mix with the crabmeat, eggs, cream, flour and 60 g (2¼ oz) of the cheese.

Fill each pastry case with crab filling and sprinkle with the remaining cheese. Place a thyme sprig over the top. Bake for 20 minutes, or until puffed and golden brown.

PREPARATION TIME: 25 MINUTES   COOKING TIME: 20 MINUTES

CHICKEN LIVER PÂTÉ WITH PISTACHIOS AND PROSCIUTTO

8–10 very thin slices prosciutto
30 g (1 oz) butter
60 ml (2 fl oz/¼ cup) olive oil
2 bacon slices, finely diced
1 onion, finely chopped
2 garlic cloves, crushed
500 g (1 lb 2 oz) chicken livers, trimmed of fat and veins
3 bay leaves
80 ml (2½ fl oz/⅓ cup) sherry or brandy
125 g (4½ oz) butter, extra, softened
50 g (1¾ oz/⅓ cup) pistachio nuts, toasted

SERVES 10

Line an 11 x 25 cm (4¼ x 10 inch) loaf (bar) tin with foil, then line with the prosciutto slices so that the prosciutto hangs over the long sides, making sure each slice overlaps slightly. Heat the butter and oil in a frying pan and cook the bacon, onion and garlic for 5 minutes, or until the onion is soft but not brown. Add the chicken livers to the pan with the bay leaves. Increase the heat to hot and cook for 3–4 minutes, or until the livers are brown on the outside, but still slightly pink on the inside.

Add the sherry to the pan and simmer, stirring constantly, for 3 minutes, or until the liquid has almost all evaporated. Remove the bay leaves. Put the mixture in a food processor and blend to a very fine texture. Gradually add the extra butter to the food processor and blend until the mixture is smooth. Season to taste, then stir in the nuts.

Spoon the mixture into the loaf tin and fold the prosciutto over the top. Cover with plastic wrap and refrigerate for at least 3 hours, or overnight. Cut into slices for serving.

PREPARATION TIME: 20 MINUTES +   COOKING TIME: 15 MINUTES

SEAFOOD PARCELS

250 g (9 oz) skinless firm white fish fillets
100 g (3½ oz) scallops
400 g (14 oz) cooked prawns (shrimp)
30 g (1 oz) butter
1 tablespoon lemon juice
1 tablespoon plain (all-purpose) flour
250 ml (9 fl oz/1 cup) milk
60 g (2¼ oz) cheddar cheese, grated
1 tablespoon snipped chives
1 tablespoon chopped dill
10 sheets filo pastry
60 g (2¼ oz) butter, melted
2 teaspoons poppy seeds or sesame seeds

MAKES 20

Preheat the oven to 180°C (350°F/Gas 4). Line a baking tray with baking paper. Cut the fish into 1 cm (½ inch) wide strips. Wash the scallops and slice or pull off any vein, membrane or hard white muscle, leaving any roe attached. Peel the prawns and gently pull out the dark vein from each prawn back, starting at the head end.

Melt the butter in a heavy-based saucepan. Add the fish, scallops and lemon juice. Cook over medium heat for 1 minute, or until tender. Remove from the pan with a slotted spoon, place in a bowl and keep warm.

Stir the flour into the butter and cook for 1 minute, or until pale and foaming. Remove from the heat and gradually stir in the milk. Return to the heat and stir constantly until the mixture boils and thickens. Reduce the heat and simmer for 2 minutes. Stir in the cheddar, chives, dill, fish, scallops and prawns. Remove from the heat and season to taste. Cover the surface with plastic wrap.

Layer two sheets of pastry together with melted butter, then cut into four equal strips. Cover the unused pastry with a damp tea towel (dish towel). Place 2 tablespoons of seafood mixture on one short end of each pastry strip. Fold in the edges and roll up. Repeat with the remaining pastry, seafood and some of the remaining butter. Place the parcels, seam side down, on the baking tray. Brush with the remaining melted butter, sprinkle with poppy seeds and bake for 20 minutes.

PREPARATION TIME: 25 MINUTES   COOKING TIME: 35 MINUTES

NOTE: You can make the sauce a day ahead and refrigerate.

BAGUETTE WITH EGG, DILL PESTO AND PROSCIUTTO

8 thin slices prosciutto
1 baguette, sliced diagonally
2 teaspoons butter
7 eggs, lightly beaten
80 ml (2½ fl oz/⅓ cup) milk
1 tablespoon light sour cream

PESTO
45 g (1¾ oz) dill
75 g (2¾ oz) pine nuts, toasted
60 g (2½ oz) parmesan cheese, finely grated
2 garlic cloves, crushed
80 ml (2½ fl oz/⅓ cup) virgin olive oil

MAKES 30

Preheat the oven to 200°C (400°F/Gas 6). Spread the prosciutto on a baking tray lined with baking paper. Bake for 5 minutes, or until lightly crisp. Set aside. Arrange the bread on baking trays and grill (broil) until golden on both sides.

To make the pesto, finely chop the dill, pine nuts, parmesan and garlic together in a food processor. With the motor running, add the oil in a thin stream and process until smooth, then season. Spread the bread with the dill pesto.

Heat the butter in a large non-stick frying pan over low heat. Add the combined egg and milk. As the egg begins to set, use a wooden spoon to scrape along the base with long strokes to bring the cooked egg to the surface in large lumps. Repeat several times over 10 minutes, or until the mixture is cooked but still creamy-looking. Remove from the heat and stir in the sour cream, then season. Divide the egg among the toasts and top with torn prosciutto. Serve immediately.

PREPARATION TIME: 20 MINUTES   COOKING TIME: 20 MINUTES

POTTED PRAWNS

250 g (9 oz) small cooked prawns
100 g (3½ oz) butter
¼ teaspoon freshly grated nutmeg
¼ teaspoon ground ginger
pinch cayenne pepper

MAKES 350 G (12 OZ/1⅓ CUPS)

Peel the prawns and gently pull out the dark vein from each prawn back, starting at the head end. Chop the prawns very finely. Melt 60 g (2¼ oz) of the butter over low heat in a small saucepan. Add the prawns, nutmeg, ginger, cayenne pepper and season to taste.

Stir over low heat for 2 minutes, or until all the butter has been absorbed into the mixture. Spoon into a 350 ml (12 fl oz) ramekin or dariole mould, press down, then smooth the surface.

Melt the remaining butter in a small saucepan and pour over the surface (leaving the white sediment behind in the pan) to cover completely. Refrigerate overnight to allow the flavours to develop. Bring back to room temperature and serve with toast.

PREPARATION TIME: 10 MINUTES +   COOKING TIME: 5 MINUTES

Baguette with egg, dill pesto and prosciutto

WARM DUCK AND CORIANDER TARTLETS

185 g (6½ oz/1½ cups) plain (all-purpose) flour
125 g (4½ oz) chilled butter, chopped
40 g (1½ oz/¼ cup) sesame seeds
2 tablespoons iced water
coriander (cilantro) sprigs, to garnish

FILLING
1 large Chinese roasted duck (see NOTES)
2 tablespoons orange marmalade
1 tablespoon kecap manis (see NOTES)
2 teaspoons sesame oil
1 tablespoon grated fresh ginger
5 spring onions (scallions), thinly sliced

MAKES 24

Lightly grease two 12-hole round-based patty pans or mini muffin tins. Sift the flour and ½ teaspoon salt into a large bowl and add the butter. Using your fingertips, rub in the butter until the mixture resembles fine breadcrumbs. Stir in the sesame seeds. Make a well in the centre and add the iced water (you may not need to use all of it) and mix with a flat-bladed knife until the dough just comes together. Turn out onto a lightly floured surface and gather into a ball.

Preheat the oven to 210°C (415°F/Gas 6–7). Roll the pastry out thinly on a lightly floured work surface until 3 mm (⅛ inch) thick. Prick lightly all over. Cut 24 rounds with a 6 cm (2½ inch) fluted cutter. Re-roll the pastry if necessary. Line the tins with pastry. Bake for 10 minutes, or until the pastry is golden brown, then remove from the tins and allow to cool.

To make the filling, remove the duck meat from the bones and shred the meat. Put the marmalade in a saucepan and stir over low heat until smooth. Add the remaining ingredients, including the shredded duck, and mix well. Stir until warmed through.

Arrange the pastry shells on a warm serving platter and add the warm filling. Garnish with the fresh coriander and serve immediately.

PREPARATION TIME: 35 MINUTES +   COOKING TIME: 15 MINUTES

NOTES: The skin from the duck can also be used in the filling. However, all visible fat should be removed.

Kecap manis is an Indonesian sweet soy sauce, available in most supermarkets. If kecap manis is not available, use soy sauce mixed with a little soft brown sugar.

GARLIC TOAST WITH SALMON MAYONNAISE

1 capsicum (pepper)
1 tomato
8 slices bread, crusts removed, cut into 4 triangles, or 1 baguette, sliced
80 ml (2½ fl oz/⅓ cup) olive oil
2 garlic cloves, crushed
2 tablespoons olive oil, extra
1 onion, finely chopped

SALMON MAYONNAISE
2 egg yolks
2 garlic cloves, crushed
2 teaspoons lemon juice
185 ml (6 fl oz/¾ cup) olive oil
60 g (2¼ oz) sliced smoked salmon

MAKES 32

Remove the seeds and membrane from the capsicum and finely chop the flesh. Score a cross in the base of the tomato. Put in a heatproof bowl and and cover with boiling water. Leave for 30 seconds, then transfer to cold water, drain and peel the skin away from the cross. Cut the tomato in half, scoop out the seeds and finely chop the flesh.

Preheat the oven to 180°C (350°F/Gas 4). Brush both sides of the bread with the combined oil and garlic and bake on a baking tray for 10–15 minutes. Turn halfway through cooking. Set aside. Heat the extra oil in a frying pan, add the capsicum, tomato and onion and fry until the onion is soft. Remove from the heat.

To make the salmon mayonnaise, whisk the egg yolks, garlic and lemon juice together in a small bowl. Beat the oil into the mixture, 1 teaspoon at a time, ensuring all the oil is combined before adding more. The mixture will have the consistency of thick cream. Transfer the mayonnaise to a food processor, add the salmon and some freshly ground pepper to taste, then process until smooth. Serve the garlic toasts topped with some capsicum mixture, then salmon mayonnaise.

PREPARATION TIME: 35 MINUTES   COOKING TIME: 30 MINUTES

CAVIAR EGGS

20 eggs
1 tablespoon curry powder
375 g (13 oz/1½ cups) whole-egg mayonnaise
45 g (1¾ oz) red caviar
45 g (1¾ oz) black caviar

MAKES 40

Put the eggs in a saucepan, cover with cold water and slowly bring to the boil. Gently stir the eggs while boiling to centre the yolk. Cook for 7 minutes, rinse under cold water and peel.

Cut the eggs in half lengthways, remove the yolks and push the yolks through a fine sieve into a bowl. Blend in the curry powder and mayonnaise, stirring until the mixture is smooth. Put the filling in a piping (icing) bag fitted with a 1 cm (½ inch) star nozzle. Pipe the mixture into the egg cavities. Garnish with red and black caviar just before serving.

PREPARATION TIME: 20 MINUTES   COOKING TIME: 10 MINUTES

Garlic toast with salmon mayonnaise

TUNA TARTLETS WITH APPLE MOUSSELINE MAYONNAISE

375 g (13 oz) tuna, in one piece, skinned
24 hard-boiled quail eggs, halved lengthways, to garnish (see NOTE)
45 g (1³/4 oz) coriander (cilantro) leaves, to garnish

CURE
500 g (1 lb 2 oz) rock salt
330 g (11³/4 oz/1¹/2 cups) sugar
¹/2 teaspoon ground black peppercorns
1 teaspoon ground ginger

FILO TARTLETS
250 g (9 oz) filo pastry
250 g (9 oz) unsalted butter, melted

APPLE MOUSSELINE MAYONNAISE
2 tablespoons smooth apple sauce
250 g (9 oz/1 cup) whole-egg mayonnaise
2 tablespoons whipped cream

MAKES ABOUT 48

Choose a large flat non-metallic dish for curing. Cut the tuna into 3 cm (1¹/4 inch) strips the length of the tuna, then cut the lengths to fit the dish.

Mix the cure ingredients and cover the base of the dish with a layer of the cure, then a layer of tuna. Continue layering, finishing with a layer of cure. Weigh down and refrigerate for 4 hours.

Remove the tuna from the cure. Wash the tuna under cold running water, then dry thoroughly. If not using right away, wrap in a lightly oiled clean cloth to prevent the tuna from drying out. Refrigerate before slicing.

Preheat the oven to 190°C (375°F/Gas 5). For the filo cups, layer six sheets of filo on top of one another, brushing each with melted butter. Keep the remainder under a damp tea towel (dish towel) until needed.

Cut 8 cm (3¹/4 inch) rounds of the layered filo with a cutter. Cut through with scissors if necessary. Line two 12-hole round-based patty pans or mini muffin tins with the rounds, butter side down. Press into the holes and prick with a fork. Arrange on baking trays and freeze for at least 10 minutes. While chilling, prepare the remaining filo rounds, but keep covered to prevent them drying out.

Bake the pastry cases for 4–5 minutes. Remove from the tins and cool on a wire rack. Repeat with the remaining filo rounds.

To make the mayonnaise, fold the apple sauce into the mayonnaise, then fold in the cream. Season to taste, if necessary.

Do not assemble until just before serving. Slice the tuna across the grain in paper-thin slices with a sharp knife. Spoon a teaspoonful of mayonnaise into each case. Top with a slice of tuna, half a quail egg and a coriander leaf. Serve at once.

PREPARATION TIME: 1 HOUR +   COOKING TIME: 10 MINUTES

NOTE: Cook quail eggs in boiling water for 5 minutes, then place in cold water to cool.

FLORENTINE SCONES WITH MORTADELLA AND ARTICHOKE

100 g (3½ oz) English spinach leaves
20 g (¾ oz) butter
3 spring onions (scallions), thinly sliced
155 g (5½ oz/1¼ cups) self-raising flour
50 g (1¾ oz) parmesan cheese, grated
80 ml (2½ fl oz/⅓ cup) milk, approximately
2 teaspoons milk, extra
200 g (7 oz) artichokes in olive oil, drained
60 ml (2 fl oz/¼ cup) thick (double/heavy) cream
100 g (3½ oz) mortadella, thinly sliced
1½ tablespoons finely chopped pistachio nuts

MAKES 60

Preheat the oven to 220°C (425°F/Gas 7). Cook the spinach, covered, in a saucepan full of water over medium heat for 2 minutes, or until wilted. Drain and cool. Squeeze the spinach with your hands to remove as much liquid as possible, then chop finely. Heat the butter in a small frying pan, add the spring onion and cook over medium heat for 2 minutes, or until very soft.

Sift the flour into a bowl and stir in the spinach, onion and parmesan. Make a well in the centre and use a flat-bladed knife to stir in enough milk to mix to a soft, sticky dough. Turn onto a lightly floured surface and knead lightly until just smooth. Roll out to about 1.5 cm (⅝ inch) thick, then cut 30 rounds with a 4 cm (1½ inch) cutter. Lightly grease a baking tray and place the rounds on it so they are almost touching. Brush the tops lightly with the extra milk and bake on the middle shelf for 10–12 minutes, or until golden brown.

Meanwhile, chop the artichokes in a food processor until smooth. Add the cream and process quickly until combined, taking care not to overprocess. Season to taste. To assemble, split the scones horizontally in half, top each half with artichoke cream, then torn and folded pieces of mortadella. Sprinkle with pistachio nuts.

PREPARATION TIME: 30 MINUTES   COOKING TIME: 15 MINUTES

LAMB ON POLENTA

750 ml (26 fl oz/3 cups) chicken stock
110 g (3¾ oz/¾ cup) instant polenta
2 tablespoons freshly grated parmesan cheese
oil, for frying
2 lamb fillets (150 g/5½ oz each), trimmed of excess fat and sinew
¼ small Lebanese (short) cucumber, thinly sliced
60 g (2¼ oz/¼ cup) plain yoghurt

MAKES 24

Lightly grease a 20 x 30 cm (8 x 12 inch) shallow tray. Pour the stock into a saucepan and bring to the boil. Add the polenta and stir over medium heat for 5 minutes, or until thick. Remove from the heat. Stir in the parmesan and season to taste. Spread into the tray, then cool. When cool, cut the polenta into rounds with a 4 cm (1½ inch) cutter.

Heat a little oil in a frying pan, add the lamb and cook until brown all over and cooked as desired — about 3 minutes each side for medium. Remove the lamb from the pan and wipe the pan clean. Add more oil to the pan and fry the polenta rounds until lightly browned on both sides. Remove from the pan. Cut the cucumber slices into quarters. Thinly slice the lamb and place on top of the polenta. Top with yoghurt and a piece of cucumber.

PREPARATION TIME: 15 MINUTES +   COOKING TIME: 15 MINUTES

QUICHE LORRAINE

PASTRY
215 g (7³/4 oz/1³/4 cups) plain (all-purpose) flour
100 g (3¹/2 oz) chilled butter, chopped
2 tablespoons iced water

30 g (1 oz) butter
1 onion, finely chopped
3 bacon slices, finely chopped
3 eggs
185 ml (6 fl oz/³/4 cup) pouring (whipping) cream
80 g (2³/4 oz) grated gruyère cheese
¹/4 teaspoon freshly grated nutmeg

SERVES 6

To make the pastry, sift the flour into a bowl and add the chilled butter. Rub the butter into the flour with your fingertips until it resembles fine breadcrumbs. Make a well in the centre and add the iced water. Mix with a flat-bladed knife, using a cutting action, until the mixture comes together in beads. Add a little more water if the dough is too dry. Turn out onto a lightly floured surface and gather into a ball. Cover with plastic wrap and refrigerate for 20 minutes.

Preheat the oven to 190°C (375°F/Gas 5). Roll out the pastry between two sheets of baking paper to fit a shallow loose-based 25 cm (10 inch) tart tin. Lift the pastry into the tin and press it well into the sides. Trim off any excess by rolling a rolling pin across the top of the tin. Refrigerate the pastry for 20 minutes. Cover the shell with baking paper, fill evenly with baking beads or uncooked rice and bake for 15 minutes, or until the pastry is dried out and golden. Cool slightly before filling. Reduce the oven temperature to 180°C (350°F/Gas 4).

Melt the butter in a frying pan and cook the onion and bacon over medium heat for 10 minutes. Cool, then spread over the cooled pastry.

Whisk together the eggs, cream and half of the gruyère cheese and season. Pour over the onion and sprinkle with the remaining gruyère and the nutmeg. Bake for 30 minutes, or until just firm.

PREPARATION TIME: 30 MINUTES +   COOKING TIME: 45 MINUTES

ROAST BEEF, PÂTÉ AND ROCKET FINGERS

16 slices bread
165 g (5³/₄ oz) cracked pepper paté
250 g (9 oz) sliced rare roast beef
165 g (5³/₄ oz) semi-dried (sun-blushed) tomatoes
rocket (arugula) leaves

MAKES 24

Trim the crusts from the bread. Spread the pâté over half the bread.

Make sandwiches using the roast beef, semi-dried tomatoes and rocket leaves. Cut each into three fingers to serve.

PREPARATION TIME: 10 MINUTES   COOKING TIME: NIL

HAM AND CORN RELISH FINGERS

butter, to spread
16 slices white bread
250 g (9 oz/1 cup) sour cream
140 g (5 oz) corn relish
8 slices dark seed bread
8 slices ham

MAKES 24

Butter eight slices of the white bread. Mix the sour cream with the corn relish and spread on the unbuttered slices of white bread. Top each with a slice of the dark seed bread. Top that with sliced ham, then sandwich with a buttered slice of white bread.

Remove the crusts and slice each sandwich into three.

PREPARATION TIME: 10 MINUTES   COOKING TIME: NIL

Roast beef, pâté and rocket fingers

SMOKED SALMON
MINI QUICHES

2 sheets ready-made shortcrust (pie) pastry
100 g (3½ oz) cream cheese
60 ml (2 fl oz/¼ cup) pouring (whipping) cream
2 eggs
100 g (3½ oz) smoked salmon, finely chopped

MAKES 24

Preheat the oven to 200°C (400°F/Gas 6). Grease two round-based shallow 12-hole patty pans or mini muffin tins. Lay the shortcrust pastry on a work surface and cut 12 rounds from each sheet with an 8 cm (3¼ inch) cutter. Line the holes with pastry.

Put the cream cheese, cream and eggs in a food processor and mix together, then season to taste with some cracked black pepper. Sprinkle the smoked salmon into the pastry cases. Pour the cream cheese mixture over the top and bake for 15–20 minutes, or until puffed and golden.

Remove from the patty pans while warm and transfer to wire racks to cool.

PREPARATION TIME: 15 MINUTES   COOKING TIME: 20 MINUTES

TRADITIONAL BITES

ENGLISH MUFFINS

2 teaspoons sachet dried yeast
$\frac{1}{2}$ teaspoon sugar
530 g (1 lb 3 oz/$4\frac{1}{4}$ cups) plain
(all-purpose) flour
350 ml (12 fl oz) lukewarm milk
1 egg, lightly beaten
40 g ($1\frac{1}{2}$ oz) butter, melted

MAKES 15

Lightly dust two 28 x 32 cm ($11\frac{1}{4}$ x $12\frac{3}{4}$ inch) baking trays with flour. Put the yeast, sugar, 1 teaspoon of the flour and 60 ml (2 fl oz/$\frac{1}{4}$ cup) warm water in a small bowl and mix well. Leave in a warm, draught-free place for 10 minutes, or until bubbles appear on the surface. The mixture should be frothy and slightly increased in volume. If your yeast doesn't foam, it is dead, so you will have to discard it and start again.

Sift the remaining flour and 1 teaspoon salt into a large bowl. Make a well in the centre and add the milk, egg, butter and yeast mixture all at once. Using a flat-bladed knife, mix to a soft dough.

Turn the dough onto a lightly floured surface and knead lightly for 2 minutes, or until smooth. Shape the dough into a ball and place in a large, lightly oiled bowl. Cover with plastic wrap or a damp tea towel (dish towel) and leave in a warm place for $1\frac{1}{2}$ hours, or until well risen.

Preheat the oven to 210°C (415°F/Gas 6-7). Punch the dough down and knead again for 2 minutes, or until smooth. Roll to 1 cm ($\frac{1}{2}$ inch) thick, then cut into rounds with a lightly floured plain 8 cm ($3\frac{1}{4}$ inch) cutter and place on the trays. Cover with plastic wrap or a damp tea towel and leave in a warm, draught-free place for 10 minutes.

Bake for 15 minutes, turning once halfway through cooking. Transfer to a wire rack to cool. Serve warm or cold.

PREPARATION TIME: 20 MINUTES +   COOKING TIME: 15 MINUTES

PUMPKIN AND SAGE SCONES

250 g (9 oz/2 cups) self-raising flour
250 g (9 oz/1 cup) cooked and puréed pumpkin (winter squash)
20 g ($^3/_4$ oz) butter
1 tablespoon chopped sage
milk

MAKES 8

Preheat the oven to 180°C (350°F/Gas 4). Lightly grease a baking tray or line with baking paper. Sift the self-raising flour into a bowl with a pinch of salt. Using your fingertips, rub the pumpkin and butter into the flour and then add the sage.

Bring the mixture together with a little milk and turn it out onto the tray. Shape the mixture into a round and roll it out to about 3 cm (1$^1/_4$ inches) thick. Gently mark or cut the scone into eight segments and bake for 15–20 minutes, or until lightly browned and cooked through.

PREPARATION TIME: 10 MINUTES   COOKING TIME: 20 MINUTES

DIGESTIVE BISCUITS

125 g (4$^1/_2$ oz) unsalted butter, softened
60 g (2$^1/_4$ oz/$^1/_3$ cup) soft brown sugar
1 tablespoon malt extract
1 egg, lightly beaten
125 g (4$^1/_2$ oz/1 cup) plain (all-purpose) flour
150 g (5$^1/_2$ oz/1 cup) wholemeal (whole-wheat) plain (all-purpose) flour
35 g (1$^1/_4$ oz/$^1/_2$ cup) unprocessed bran
1 teaspoon baking powder

MAKES 16

Line two baking trays with baking paper. Cream the butter, sugar and malt extract in a small bowl using electric beaters until light and fluffy. Gradually add the egg, beating thoroughly after each addition. Transfer to a large bowl.

Sift the flours, bran and baking powder into a small bowl, returning the husks to the bowl. Using a large metal spoon, fold in the dry ingredients in three portions and mix to a firm dough. Cover and refrigerate for at least 1 hour.

Preheat the oven to 180°C (350°F/Gas 4). Roll out half the dough between two sheets of baking paper to 5 mm ($^1/_4$ inch) thick. Cut out rounds using a 7 cm (2$^3/_4$ inch) plain cutter and place the rounds on the trays. Repeat with the remaining dough and re-roll any scraps. Refrigerate for 20 minutes.

Bake for 12 minutes, or until golden brown and firm. Leave on the trays to cool slightly before transferring to a wire rack to cool completely. When the biscuits (cookies) are cold, store them in an airtight container.

PREPARATION TIME: 15 MINUTES +   COOKING TIME: 12 MINUTES

NOTE: Digestives can be eaten plain but are delicious buttered or served with cheese. They can also be drizzled with melted chocolate.

Pumpkin and sage scones

SCONES

310 g (11 oz/2½ cups) self-raising flour
1 teaspoon baking powder
40 g (1½ oz) chilled unsalted butter, cubed
1 tablespoon sugar
250 ml (9 fl oz/1 cup) milk

MAKES 10–12

Preheat the oven to 220°C (425°F/Gas 7). Lightly grease a baking tray or line with baking paper.

Sift the flour, baking powder and a pinch of salt into a bowl. Using your fingertips, rub in the butter briefly and lightly until the mixture resembles fine breadcrumbs. Mix in the sugar. Make a well in the centre. Pour in almost all the milk and mix with a flat-bladed knife, using a cutting action, until the dough comes together in clumps. Rotate the bowl as you work. Use the remaining milk if the mixture seems dry. Handle the mixture with great care and a very light hand. The dough should feel slightly wet and sticky. With floured hands, gently gather the dough together, lift onto a lightly floured surface and pat into a smooth ball. Do not knead or the scones will be tough.

Pat or lightly roll the dough out to 2 cm (¾ inch) thick. Using a floured 6 cm (2½ inch) cutter, cut into rounds. Don't pat out too thinly or the scones will not be a good height. Gather the scraps together and, without over-handling, press out as before and cut out more rounds. Place close together on the baking tray and lightly brush the tops with milk.

Bake in the top half of the oven for 12–15 minutes, or until risen and golden. If you aren't sure they are cooked, break one open. If still doughy in the centre, cook for a few more minutes. For soft scones, wrap them in a dry tea towel (dish towel) while hot. For scones with a crisp top, transfer to a wire rack to cool slightly before wrapping. Serve warm or at room temperature, with butter or jam and whipped or clotted cream.

PREPARATION TIME: 20 MINUTES   COOKING TIME: 15 MINUTES

COCONUT JAM SLICE

125 g (4¹/₂ oz/1 cup) plain (all-purpose) flour
60 g (2¹/₄ oz/¹/₂ cup) self-raising flour
150 g (5¹/₂ oz) unsalted butter, cubed
60 g (2¹/₄ oz/¹/₂ cup) icing (confectioners') sugar
1 egg yolk
160 g (5³/₄ oz/¹/₂ cup) strawberry jam
125 g (4¹/₂ oz) caster (superfine) sugar
3 eggs
270 g (9¹/₂ oz/3 cups) desiccated coconut

MAKES 20

Preheat the oven to 180°C (350°F/Gas 4). Lightly grease a shallow 23 cm (9 inch) square tin and line with baking paper, leaving the paper hanging over on two opposite sides.

Put the flours, butter and icing sugar together in a food processor and mix in short bursts until the mixture is fine and crumbly. Add the egg yolk and process until the mixture just comes together. Alternatively, put the flour and icing sugar in a bowl and rub in the butter with your fingertips until the mixture is fine and crumbly. Mix in the egg yolk and then gather together. Press the dough into the tin and refrigerate for 10 minutes. Bake for 15 minutes, or until golden brown. Allow to cool, then spread the jam evenly over the pastry.

Beat the caster sugar and eggs together in a small bowl until creamy, then stir in the coconut. Spread the mixture over the jam, gently pressing down with the back of a spoon. Bake for 25–30 minutes, or until lightly golden. Leave to cool in the tin, then lift the slice out, using the paper as handles. Cut the slice into pieces. Store in an airtight container for up to 4 days.

PREPARATION TIME: 30 MINUTES +   COOKING TIME: 45 MINUTES

BROWN SUGAR SHORTBREAD

250 g (9 oz) unsalted butter, softened
140 g (5 oz/³/₄ cup) soft brown sugar
250 g (9 oz/2 cups) plain (all-purpose) flour
90 g (3¹/₄ oz/¹/₂ cup) rice flour
¹/₂ teaspoon ground mixed (pumpkin pie) spice

MAKES 50

Preheat the oven to 160°C (315°F/Gas 2–3). Line two baking trays with baking paper. Cream the butter and sugar in a small bowl using electric beaters until light and fluffy. Add the sifted flours, mixed spice and a pinch of salt and mix with a knife, using a cutting action, to a soft dough. Gather together and gently knead for 1 minute. Refrigerate in plastic wrap for 20 minutes.

Divide the mixture into four, gently knead, then roll a portion onto a lightly floured surface to 5 mm (¹/₄ inch) thick. Cut out shapes with a 4–5 cm (1¹/₂–2 inch) biscuit (cookie) cutter, or cut into 5 cm (2 inch) rounds. Re-roll the trimmings and repeat the process with the remaining portions of dough.

Place the shortbreads on the trays and bake for 15–20 minutes, or until lightly golden and firm to the touch. Remove from the oven and leave on the trays to cool for 2 minutes before transferring to a wire rack to cool completely. When cold, store in an airtight container.

PREPARATION TIME: 25 MINUTES +   COOKING TIME: 20 MINUTES

VANILLA SLICE

500 g (1 lb 2 oz) block ready-made puff pastry, thawed
230 g (8¹/₂ oz/1 cup) caster (superfine) sugar
90 g (3¹/₄ oz/³/₄ cup) cornflour (cornstarch)
60 g (2¹/₄ oz/¹/₂ cup) custard powder or instant vanilla pudding mix
1 litre (35 fl oz/4 cups) pouring (whipping) cream
60 g (2¹/₄ oz) unsalted butter, cubed
2 teaspoons natural vanilla extract
3 egg yolks

ICING
185 g (6¹/₂ oz/1¹/₂ cups) icing (confectioners') sugar
60 g (2¹/₄ oz) passionfruit pulp
15 g (¹/₂ oz) unsalted butter, melted

MAKES 9

Preheat the oven to 210°C (415°F/Gas 6–7). Grease two baking trays with oil. Line the base and sides of a shallow 23 cm (9 inch) square cake tin with foil, leaving the foil hanging over on two opposite sides. Divide the pastry in half, roll each piece to a 25 cm (10 inch) square about 3 mm (¹/₈ inch) thick and place each one on a prepared tray. Prick all over with a fork and bake for 8 minutes, or until golden. Trim each pastry sheet to a 23 cm (9 inch) square. Place one sheet, top side down, in the cake tin.

Combine the sugar, cornflour and custard powder in a saucepan. Gradually add the cream and stir until smooth. Place over medium heat and stir constantly for 2 minutes, or until the mixture boils and thickens. Add the butter and vanilla and stir until smooth. Remove from the heat and whisk in the egg yolks until combined. Spread the custard over the pastry in the tin and cover with the remaining pastry, top side down. Allow to cool.

To make the icing (frosting), combine the icing sugar, passionfruit pulp and butter in a small bowl and stir together until smooth.

Lift the slice out, using the foil as handles, spread the icing over the top and leave it to set before carefully cutting into squares with a serrated knife.

PREPARATION TIME: 40 MINUTES   COOKING TIME: 15 MINUTES

MELTING MOMENTS

250 g (9 oz) unsalted butter, softened
40 g (1½ oz/⅓ cup) icing (confectioners')
sugar
1 teaspoon natural vanilla extract
185 g (6½ oz/1½ cups) self-raising flour
60 g (2¼ oz/½ cup) custard powder or
instant vanilla pudding mix

PASSIONFRUIT FILLING
60 g (2¼ oz) unsalted butter
60 g (2¼ oz/½ cup) icing (confectioners')
sugar
1½ tablespoons passionfruit pulp

MAKES 14

Preheat the oven to 180°C (350°F/Gas 4). Line two baking trays with baking paper.

Cream the butter and icing sugar in a bowl using electric beaters until light and fluffy, then beat in the vanilla. Sift in the flour and custard powder and mix with a flat-bladed knife, using a cutting motion, to form a soft dough.

Roll level tablespoons of dough into balls (you should have 28) and place on the trays, leaving room for spreading. Flatten slightly with a floured fork. Bake for 20 minutes, or until lightly golden. Cool slightly on the trays before transferring to a wire rack to cool completely.

To make the passionfruit filling, beat the butter and sugar in a bowl using electric beaters until light and creamy, then beat in the passionfruit pulp. Use to sandwich the biscuits together. Leave to firm before serving.

PREPARATION TIME: 40 MINUTES +   COOKING TIME: 20 MINUTES

COFFEE KISSES

375 g (13 oz/3 cups) self-raising flour
160 g (5¾ oz) unsalted butter, chopped
115 g (4 oz/½ cup) caster (superfine) sugar
1 egg, lightly beaten
1 tablespoon instant coffee powder
1–2 tablespoons iced water

COFFEE BUTTERCREAM
80 g (2¾ oz) unsalted butter
125 g (4½ oz/1 cup) icing (confectioners')
sugar, sifted
2 teaspoons instant coffee powder, mixed
with 2 teaspoons water
100 g (3½ oz) white chocolate, melted
chocolate-coated coffee beans (optional)

MAKES 30

Preheat the oven to 180°C (350°F/Gas 4). Brush two baking trays with oil, then line with baking paper. Sift the flour into a bowl. Add the butter and rub into the flour, using your fingertips, until the mixture resembles fine breadcrumbs. Add the combined sugar, egg, and coffee powder dissolved in the iced water, all at once. Mix with a knife until the ingredients come together to form a soft dough. Lightly knead until smooth. Roll out between two sheets of baking paper to 5 mm (¼ inch) thick. Cut into 5 cm (2 inch) rounds, using a fluted biscuit (cookie) cutter. Place on the trays. Bake for 10 minutes or until lightly golden. Transfer to a wire rack to cool.

To make the buttercream, beat the butter and icing sugar using electric beaters until light and creamy. Add the coffee powder mixture and beat until mixed. Place in a piping (icing) bag fitted with a fluted nozzle and pipe onto half of the biscuits. Top with another biscuit, then sandwich together. Drizzle or pipe with the melted chocolate. Top each with a chocolate-coated coffee bean, if desired.

PREPARATION TIME: 40 MINUTES +   COOKING TIME: 10 MINUTES

LEBKUCHEN

290 g (10 1/4 oz/2 1/3 cups) plain (all-purpose) flour
60 g (2 1/4 oz/1/2 cup) cornflour (cornstarch)
2 teaspoons unsweetened cocoa powder
1 teaspoon ground mixed (pumpkin pie) spice
1 teaspoon ground cinnamon
1/2 teaspoon freshly grated nutmeg
100 g (3 1/2 oz) unsalted butter, cubed
260 g (9 1/4 oz/3/4 cup) golden syrup or dark corn syrup
2 tablespoons milk
150 g (5 1/2 oz/1 cup) white chocolate melts
1/4 teaspoon ground mixed (pumpkin pie) spice, extra, to sprinkle

MAKES 35

Preheat the oven to 180°C (350°F/Gas 4). Line two baking trays with baking paper.

Sift the flours, cocoa powder and spices into a large bowl and make a well in the centre.

Place the butter, golden syrup and milk in a small saucepan, and stir over low heat until the butter has melted and the mixture is smooth. Remove from the heat and add to the dry ingredients. Using a flat-bladed knife, mix with a cutting action until the mixture comes together in small beads. Gather together with your hands and turn out onto a sheet of baking paper.

Roll the dough out to 8 mm (3/8 inch) thick. Cut into heart shapes using a 6 cm (2 1/2 inch) biscuit (cookie) cutter. Place on the trays and bake for 25 minutes, or until lightly browned. Leave on the trays to cool slightly before transferring to a wire rack to cool completely.

Place the chocolate in a small heatproof bowl. Bring a saucepan of water to the boil, then remove from the heat. Sit the bowl over the pan, making sure the base of the bowl does not touch the water. Stir occasionally until the chocolate has melted.

Dip one half of each biscuit into the chocolate and place on a sheet of baking paper until the chocolate has set. Sprinkle the un-iced side of the biscuits with mixed spice. These biscuits can be stored in an airtight container for up to 5 days.

PREPARATION TIME: 25 MINUTES +   COOKING TIME: 30 MINUTES

CUSTARD ROLLS

375 ml (13 fl oz/1½ cups) milk
115 g (4 oz/½ cup) caster (superfine) sugar
60 g (2¼ oz/½ cup) semolina
1 teaspoon grated lemon zest
1 egg, lightly beaten
12 sheets filo pastry
125 g (4½ oz) unsalted butter, melted
2 tablespoons icing (confectioners') sugar
½ teaspoon ground cinnamon

MAKES 18

Put the milk, caster sugar, semolina and lemon zest in a saucepan and stir until coming to the boil. Reduce the heat and simmer for 3 minutes.

Remove from the heat and gradually whisk in the egg. Pour the custard into a bowl, cover the surface with plastic wrap and set aside to cool. Preheat the oven to 180°C (350°F/Gas 4). Lightly brush two baking trays with melted butter.

Work with two sheets of pastry at a time. Cover the rest with a tea towel (dish towel). Brush one with melted butter, then top with another. Cut lengthways into three strips. Brush the edges with melted butter.

Spoon about 1 tablespoon of the custard 5 cm (2 inches) in from the short edge of each pastry strip. Roll the pastry over the filling, fold the ends in, then roll up. Repeat with the remaining pastry and custard. Arrange on the trays 2 cm (¾ inch) apart. Brush with the remaining butter. Bake for 12–15 minutes, or until crisp and golden. Cool on a wire rack. Dust with a little of the combined icing sugar and cinnamon.

PREPARATION TIME: 35 MINUTES   COOKING TIME: 20 MINUTES

ROCK CAKES

250 g (9 oz/2 cups) self-raising flour
90 g (3¼ oz) unsalted butter, chilled and cubed
115 g (4 oz/½ cup) caster (superfine) sugar
95 g (3½ oz/½ cup) mixed dried fruit
½ teaspoon ground ginger
1 egg
60 ml (2 fl oz/¼ cup) milk

MAKES ABOUT 20

Preheat the oven to 200°C (400°F/Gas 6). Grease two baking trays. Sift the flour into a large bowl and rub in the butter with your fingertips until the mixture resembles fine breadcrumbs. Stir in the sugar, fruit and ginger.

Whisk the egg into the milk in a bowl, add to the dry ingredients and mix to a stiff dough. Drop rough heaps of mixture, about 3 tablespoons at a time, onto the trays. Bake for 10–15 minutes, or until golden. Cool on a wire rack.

PREPARATION TIME: 15 MINUTES   COOKING TIME: 15 MINUTES

NEENISH TARTS

2 tablespoons plain (all-purpose) flour
70 g (2½ oz/⅔ cup) ground almonds
60 g (2¼ oz/½ cup) icing (confectioners')
sugar, sifted
1 egg white, lightly beaten

CREAMY FILLING

1 tablespoon plain (all-purpose) flour
125 ml (4 fl oz/½ cup) milk
2 egg yolks
60 g (2¼ oz) unsalted butter, softened
2 tablespoons caster (superfine) sugar
¼ teaspoon natural vanilla extract

ICING

125 g (4½ oz/1 cup) icing (confectioners')
sugar
2 tablespoons milk, extra
1 tablespoon unsweetened cocoa powder

MAKES 12

Lightly grease a 12-hole shallow patty pan or mini muffin tin. Sift the flour into a bowl and stir in the ground almonds and icing sugar. Make a well in the centre, add the beaten egg white and mix with a flat-bladed knife, using a cutting action, until the mixture comes together in beads and forms a stiff paste. Turn onto a lightly floured surface and gently gather into a ball. Wrap in plastic wrap and refrigerate for 30 minutes, to firm.

Preheat the oven to 190°C (375°F/Gas 5). Roll out the dough between two sheets of baking paper to 3 mm (⅛ inch) thick. Cut the pastry into 12 circles with a 7 cm (2¾ inch) fluted cutter. Press the pastry circles into the greased patty pan and prick evenly with a fork. Bake for 10 minutes, or until lightly golden.

To make the filling, stir the flour and milk in a saucepan until smooth, then stir over medium heat for 2 minutes, or until the mixture boils and thickens. Remove from the heat, then quickly stir in the egg yolks until smooth. Cover the surface with plastic wrap and set aside to cool. Using electric beaters, beat the butter, sugar and vanilla in a bowl until light and creamy. Gradually add the cooled egg mixture and beat until smooth.

Spoon some of the mixture into each pastry shell and gently smooth the tops with the back of a spoon.

To make the icing (frosting), combine the icing sugar and milk in a heatproof bowl, place over a saucepan of simmering water, making sure that the base of the bowl does not touch the water, and stir until smooth and glossy. Remove, transfer half the icing to a small bowl, add the cocoa and stir until smooth.

Using a small, flat-bladed knife, spread plain icing over half of each tart, starting from the centre and making a straight line with the icing, then pushing the icing out to the edge. Allow to set. Reheat the chocolate icing and ice the other half of each tart. Allow the icing to set completely before serving.

PREPARATION TIME: 1 HOUR +   COOKING TIME: 15 MINUTES

GINGERNUTS

250 g (9 oz/2 cups) plain (all-purpose)
flour
$^1/_2$ teaspoon bicarbonate of soda
(baking soda)
1 tablespoon ground ginger
$^1/_2$ teaspoon ground mixed (pumpkin pie)
spice
125 g (4$^1/_2$ oz) unsalted butter, chopped
185 g (6$^1/_2$ oz/1 cup) soft brown sugar
60 ml (2 fl oz/$^1/_4$ cup) boiling water
1 tablespoon golden syrup or dark
corn syrup

MAKES 50

Preheat the oven to 180°C (350°F/Gas 4). Line two baking trays with baking paper. Sift the flour, bicarbonate of soda, ginger and mixed spice into a large bowl. Add the butter and sugar and rub into the flour with your fingertips until the mixture resembles fine breadcrumbs. Pour the boiling water into a small heatproof bowl, add the golden syrup and stir until dissolved. Add to the flour and mix to a soft dough with a flat-bladed knife.

Roll into balls using 2 heaped teaspoons of mixture at a time. Place on the trays, allowing room for spreading, and flatten out slightly with your fingertips. Bake for 15 minutes, or until well-coloured and firm. Cool on the trays for 10 minutes before transferring to a wire rack to cool completely. Repeat with the remaining mixture. When cold, store in an airtight container.

PREPARATION TIME: 15 MINUTES   COOKING TIME: 15 MINUTES

NOTE: Make icing (frosting) by combining 2–3 teaspoons lemon juice, 60 g (2$^1/_4$ oz/$^1/_2$ cup) sifted icing (confectioners') sugar and 10 g ($^1/_4$ oz) melted unsalted butter in a bowl. Mix until smooth, then spread over the biscuits and allow to set.

ANZAC BISCUITS

125 g (4$^1/_2$ oz/1 cup) plain (all-purpose)
flour
140 g (5 oz/$^2/_3$ cup) sugar
100 g (3$^1/_2$ oz/1 cup) rolled (porridge) oats
90 g (3$^1/_4$ oz/1 cup) desiccated coconut
125 g (4$^1/_2$ oz) unsalted butter, cubed
90 g (3$^1/_4$ oz/$^1/_4$ cup) golden syrup
or dark corn syrup
$^1/_2$ teaspoon bicarbonate of soda
(baking soda)
1 tablespoon boiling water

MAKES 26

Preheat the oven to 180°C (350°F/Gas 4). Line two baking trays with baking paper. Sift the flour into a large bowl. Add the sugar, oats and coconut and make a well in the centre. Put the butter and golden syrup in a small saucepan and stir over low heat until the butter has melted and the mixture is smooth. Remove from the heat. Dissolve the bicarbonate of soda in the boiling water and add immediately to the butter mixture. It will foam up instantly. Pour into the well in the dry ingredients and stir with a wooden spoon until well combined.

Drop level tablespoons of mixture onto the trays, allowing room for spreading. Gently flatten each biscuit with your fingertips. Bake for 20 minutes, or until just browned, leave on the tray to cool slightly, then transfer to a wire rack to cool completely. Store in an airtight container.

PREPARATION TIME: 15 MINUTES   COOKING TIME: 25 MINUTES

BRANDY SNAPS

60 g (2¼ oz) unsalted butter
2 tablespoons golden syrup or dark corn syrup
60 g (2¼ oz/⅓ cup) soft brown sugar
30 g (1 oz/¼ cup) plain (all-purpose) flour
1½ teaspoons ground ginger
60 g (2¼ oz) dark chocolate, chopped

MAKES 15

Preheat the oven to 180°C (350°F/Gas 4). Line two baking trays with baking paper. Place the butter, golden syrup and sugar in a small saucepan and stir over low heat until the butter has melted and the sugar has dissolved. Remove from the heat and add the sifted flour and ground ginger to the saucepan. Use a wooden spoon to stir the mixture until the ingredients are well combined, taking care not to overbeat.

For each brandy snap, drop 3 level teaspoons of the mixture onto each tray about 12 cm (4½ inches) apart. Bake for 5–6 minutes, or until lightly browned. Leave the biscuits (cookies) on the trays for 30 seconds then, while still hot, lift one biscuit off the tray, using a large flat knife or spatula, and wrap around the handle of a thin wooden spoon. Slide the biscuit off the spoon and set aside to cool while you curl the remaining brandy snaps.

Put the chopped chocolate in a heatproof bowl. Bring a saucepan of water to the boil, remove from the heat and place the bowl over the water, making sure the base of the bowl does not touch the water. Stir occasionally until the chocolate has melted.

Dip both ends of each brandy snap in the melted chocolate and leave to dry on a foil-lined tray.

PREPARATION TIME: 30 MINUTES   COOKING TIME: 15 MINUTES

NOTE: There is a real art to making these biscuits: work quickly, as they harden and crack when cooled. If they cool too much, return them to the oven for a few minutes to warm, then try again.

MADELEINES

125 g (4¹/₂ oz/1 cup) plain (all-purpose) flour
2 eggs
170 g (6 oz/³/₄ cup) caster (superfine) sugar
185 g (6¹/₂ oz) unsalted butter, melted and cooled
1 teaspoon finely grated orange zest
2 tablespoons icing (confectioners') sugar, to dust

MAKES 12

Preheat the oven to 180°C (350°F/Gas 4). Lightly grease a 12-hole madeleine tin or shallow patty pan. Lightly dust the madeleine tin with flour and shake off any excess.

Sift the flour three times onto baking paper. Combine the eggs and sugar in a heatproof bowl. Place the bowl over a saucepan of simmering water, making sure the base of the bowl does not touch the water, and beat the mixture using a whisk or electric beaters until thick and pale yellow. Remove the bowl from the heat and continue to beat the mixture until cooled slightly and increased in volume.

Add the sifted flour, butter and orange zest to the bowl and fold in quickly and lightly with a metal spoon until just combined. Spoon the mixture carefully into the madeleine holes. Bake for 10–12 minutes, or until lightly golden. Carefully remove from the tin and transfer to a wire rack to cool. Dust with icing sugar before serving. Madeleines are best eaten on the day of baking.

PREPARATION TIME: 20 MINUTES   COOKING TIME: 15 MINUTES

FLORENTINES

55 g (2 oz) unsalted butter
45 g (1³/₄ oz/¹/₄ cup) soft brown sugar
2 teaspoons honey
25 g (1 oz/¹/₄ cup) flaked almonds, roughly chopped
2 tablespoons chopped dried apricots
2 tablespoons chopped glacé cherries
2 tablespoons mixed peel (mixed candied citrus peel)
40 g (1¹/₂ oz/¹/₃ cup) plain (all-purpose) flour, sifted
120 g (4¹/₄ oz) dark chocolate, broken into small pieces

MAKES 12

Preheat the oven to 180°C (350°F/Gas 4). Line two large baking trays with baking paper. Place the butter, sugar and honey in a saucepan and stir over low heat until the butter is melted and all the ingredients are combined. Remove from the heat and add the almonds, apricots, glacé cherries, mixed peel and flour. Mix well.

Place level tablespoons of the mixture well apart on the trays. Flatten the biscuits into 5 cm (2 inch) rounds, then gently reshape before cooking. Bake for 10 minutes, or until lightly browned. Cool slightly on the tray before transferring to a wire rack to cool completely.

Put the dark chocolate in a heatproof bowl. Bring a small saucepan of water to the boil, remove from the heat and place the bowl over the pan, making sure the base of the bowl does not touch the water. Stir until melted. Spread on the base of each florentine and, using a fork, make a wavy pattern on the chocolate before it sets. Let the chocolate set before serving.

PREPARATION TIME: 25 MINUTES +   COOKING TIME: 15 MINUTES

LAMINGTONS

185 g (6½ oz/1½ cups) self-raising flour
40 g (1½ oz/⅓ cup) cornflour (cornstarch)
185 g (6½ oz) unsalted butter, softened
230 g (8½ oz/1 cup) caster (superfine) sugar
2 teaspoons natural vanilla extract
3 eggs, lightly beaten
125 ml (4 fl oz/½ cup) milk
185 ml (6 fl oz/¾ cup) thick (double/heavy) cream

ICING
500 g (1 lb 2 oz/4 cups) icing (confectioners') sugar
40 g (1½ oz/⅓ cup) unsweetened cocoa powder
30 g (1 oz) unsalted butter, melted
170 ml (5½ fl oz/⅔ cup) milk
270 g (9½ oz/3 cups) desiccated coconut

MAKES 16

Preheat the oven to 180°C (350°F/Gas 4). Lightly grease a shallow 23 cm (9 inch) square cake tin and line the base and sides with baking paper.

Sift the flour and cornflour into a large bowl. Add the butter, sugar, vanilla, egg and milk. Using electric beaters, beat on low speed for 1 minute, or until the ingredients are just moistened. Increase the speed to high and beat for 3 minutes, or until free of lumps and increased in volume. Pour into the tin and smooth the surface. Bake for 50–55 minutes, or until a skewer inserted into the centre of the cake comes out clean. Leave in the tin for 3 minutes before turning out onto a wire rack to cool.

Using a serrated knife, trim the top of the cake until flat. Trim the crusts from the sides, then cut the cake in half horizontally. Using electric beaters, beat the cream in a small bowl until stiff peaks form. Place the first layer of cake on a board and spread it evenly with cream. Place the remaining cake layer on top. Cut the cake into 16 squares.

To make the icing (frosting), sift the icing sugar and cocoa into a heatproof bowl and add the butter and milk. Stand the bowl over a saucepan of simmering water and stir, making sure the base of the bowl does not touch the water, until the icing is smooth and glossy, then remove from the heat. Place 90 g (3¼ oz/1 cup) of the coconut on a sheet of baking paper. Using two forks, roll a piece of cake in chocolate icing, then hold the cake over a bowl and allow the excess to drain. (Add 1 tablespoon boiling water to the icing if it seems too thick.) Roll the cake in coconut, then place on a wire rack. Repeat with the remaining cake, adding extra coconut for rolling as needed.

PREPARATION TIME: 50 MINUTES   COOKING TIME: 1 HOUR

NOTES: If you cook the cake a day ahead, it will be easier to cut and won't crumble as much.

Lamingtons are not necessarily cream filled, so if you prefer, you can ice unfilled squares of cake.

FRUIT MINCE SLICE

250 g (9 oz/2 cups) plain (all-purpose) flour
60 g (2¼ oz/½ cup) icing (confectioners') sugar
185 g (6½ oz) unsalted butter, cubed
1 egg
410 g (14½ oz) fruit mince (mincemeat)
150 g (5½ oz) pitted prunes, chopped
100 g (3½ oz) glacé ginger, chopped
1 egg, lightly beaten
icing (confectioners') sugar, extra, to dust

MAKES 15

Preheat the oven to 190°C (375°F/Gas 5). Lightly grease a shallow 18 x 28 cm (7 x 11¼ inch) tin and line the base with baking paper, leaving the paper hanging over the two long sides. Sift the flour and icing sugar into a large bowl. Rub in the butter with your fingertips until the mixture resembles fine breadcrumbs. Make a well in the centre and add the egg. Mix with a flat-bladed knife, using a cutting action, until the mixture comes together. Turn onto a lightly floured surface and press together until smooth.

Divide the dough in half and press one portion into the tin. Bake for 10 minutes, then leave to cool. Roll the remaining pastry out on a piece of baking paper and refrigerate for 15 minutes. Spread the fruit mince evenly over the baked pastry, topping with the prunes and ginger. Cut the rolled pastry into thin strips with a sharp knife or fluted pastry wheel. Arrange on top of the fruit in a diagonal lattice pattern. Brush with the beaten egg. Bake for 30 minutes, or until golden. Cool in the tin, then lift out, using the paper as handles, and cut into squares or fingers. Serve dusted with icing sugar. The slice can be kept for up to 4 days if stored in an airtight container in a cool place, or in the refrigerator.

PREPARATION TIME: 20 MINUTES +   COOKING TIME: 40 MINUTES

PARKIN

150 g (5½ oz) unsalted butter, cubed
140 g (5 oz/¾ cup) dark brown sugar
175 g (6 oz/½ cup) treacle or molasses
200 g (7 oz/2 cups) rolled (porridge) oats
125 g (4½ oz/1 cup) plain (all-purpose) flour
1 teaspoon bicarbonate of soda (baking soda)
1 tablespoon ground ginger
2 teaspoons ground mixed (pumpkin pie) spice
125 ml (4 fl oz/½ cup) milk
2 tablespoons rolled (porridge) oats, extra
2 tablespoons raw sugar

MAKES 25

Preheat the oven to 180°C (350°F/Gas 4). Lightly grease a shallow 23 cm (9 inch) square tin and line with baking paper, leaving the paper hanging over on two opposite sides.

Put the butter, brown sugar and treacle in a saucepan and stir over low heat until the butter and sugar have melted. Remove from the heat. Roughly chop the oats in a food processor, then transfer to a large bowl. Add the sifted flour, bicarbonate of soda, ginger and mixed spice. Stir in the treacle mixture and milk and mix well. Pour into the tin. Mix the extra rolled oats with the raw sugar and sprinkle over the top.

Bake for 40 minutes, or until a skewer inserted into the centre comes out clean. Leave in the tin for 5 minutes before turning out onto a wire rack to cool completely. Cut into pieces for serving. Store for up to a week in an airtight container.

PREPARATION TIME: 20 MINUTES   COOKING TIME: 45 MINUTES

SALLY LUNN BREAD

2 teaspoons dried yeast
1 teaspoon caster (superfine) sugar
3 eggs, at room temperature
185 ml (6 fl oz/^{3}/$_4$ cup) milk, warmed
115 g (4 oz/^{1}/$_3$ cup) honey
125 g (4^1/$_2$ oz) butter, melted
500 g (1 lb 2 oz/4 cups) plain (all-purpose) flour
1 tablespoon sugar, extra
1 tablespoon milk, extra

SERVES 8

Grease a deep 25 cm (10 inch) round tin and line the base with baking paper. Place the yeast, sugar and 60 ml (2 fl oz/^{1}/$_4$ cup) warm water in a small bowl and stir well. Leave in a warm, draught-free place for 10 minutes, or until bubbles appear on the surface. The mixture should be frothy and slightly increased in volume. If your yeast doesn't foam, it is dead, so you will have to discard it and start again.

Preheat the oven to 180°C (350°F/Gas 4). Place the eggs, milk, honey, butter, ^{1}/$_2$ teaspoon salt, 250 g (9 oz/2 cups) of the flour and the yeast mixture in a large bowl. Using electric beaters, beat at medium speed for 5 minutes, then stir in enough of the remaining flour to make a thick batter. Cover loosely with plastic wrap and leave in a warm place for 1–1^1/$_2$ hours, or until well risen. Stir down the batter.

Spoon the batter into the tin with a ladle or spoon, then flatten the surface of the batter with lightly oiled hands. Cover and leave to rise again for 1 hour, or until the batter reaches the top of the tin.

Bake for 35–40 minutes, or until a skewer inserted into the centre of the bread comes out clean. Brush with the combined extra sugar and milk, then return to the oven for 5 minutes. Turn out onto a wire rack and leave for 20 minutes. Slice and serve while still warm.

PREPARATION TIME: 35 MINUTES +   COOKING TIME: 45 MINUTES

NOTE: Sally Lunn bread is a cake-like bread that is often served for afternoon tea. It is traditionally served in the following way. Leave the bread to cool, then slice it horizontally into three equal layers. Toast and butter each side, then reassemble into the original bun shape. It is then sliced for serving, as shown. It can also be simply sliced in the same way you usually slice bread. It keeps for up to 5 days in an airtight container and can be frozen for up to a month.

ECCLES CAKES

150 g (5¹/₂ oz/1 cup) currants
95 g (3¹/₂ oz/¹/₂ cup) mixed peel (mixed candied citrus peel)
1 tablespoon brandy
1 tablespoon sugar
¹/₂ teaspoon ground cinnamon
500 g (1 lb 2 oz) block ready-made puff pastry, thawed
1 egg white
2 teaspoons sugar, extra, to sprinkle

MAKES 27

Preheat the oven to 210°C (415°F/Gas 6–7). Lightly grease two baking trays. To make the filling, combine the currants, peel, brandy, sugar and cinnamon in a bowl. Divide the pastry into three and roll each piece out to a thickness of 3 mm (¹/₈ inch). Using an 8 cm (3¹/₄ inch) scone cutter, cut nine circles from each sheet of pastry. (Any remaining pastry can be frozen.) Place 2 level teaspoons of the filling on each circle. Bring the edges of the rounds up together and pinch to seal. Turn, seam side down, and roll out to 1 cm (¹/₂ inch) thick ovals. Place on the trays. Brush the tops with egg white and sprinkle with extra sugar. Make three slashes across the top of each cake. Bake for 15–20 minutes, or until golden. Serve warm.

PREPARATION TIME: 20 MINUTES   COOKING TIME: 20 MINUTES

FIG NEWTONS

75 g (2³/₄ oz) unsalted butter, softened
2 tablespoons sour cream
140 g (5 oz/³/₄ cup) soft brown sugar
1 teaspoon natural vanilla extract
2 eggs, lightly beaten
375 g (13 oz/3 cups) plain (all-purpose) flour
2 teaspoons baking powder
¹/₂ teaspoon bicarbonate of soda (baking soda)
¹/₂ teaspoon ground cinnamon

FIG FILLING
375 g (13 oz) dried figs, stems removed
80 g (2³/₄ oz/¹/₃ cup) caster (superfine) sugar
1 teaspoon grated lemon zest

MAKES 24

Cream the butter, sour cream, sugar and vanilla in a small bowl using electric beaters until light and fluffy. Gradually add the egg, beating thoroughly after each addition. The mixture will appear curdled. Transfer to a large bowl and fold in the combined sifted flour, baking powder, bicarbonate of soda and cinnamon. The mixture will be very soft. Wrap in a sheet of floured plastic wrap and refrigerate for at least 2 hours. To make the filling, place the figs and 250 ml (9 fl oz/1 cup) water in a large saucepan. Bring to the boil, reduce the heat and simmer, covered, for 30 minutes, or until the figs are soft. Add the sugar and lemon zest, and simmer for 10 minutes. Cool, then drain off any remaining syrup and chop the figs in a food processor until smooth. Set aside to cool.

Preheat the oven to 180°C (350°F/Gas 4). Line a baking tray with baking paper. Divide the dough into three portions. Refrigerate two and roll the other portion on a floured surface to measure 12 x 28 cm (4¹/₂ x 11¹/₄ inches). Spread a third of the filling lengthways along one half of the pastry, leaving a 2 cm (³/₄ inch) border on that side and on the ends. Brush the border with water. Fold the unfilled half over the filling and press around the edges. Trim 1 cm (¹/₂ inch) from the side and ends to neaten. Lift onto the tray and refrigerate. Repeat with the remaining dough. Lay the three rolls on the tray, allowing room for spreading. Bake for 25 minutes, or until cooked and golden. Cool for 5 minutes on a wire rack, then trim the ends and cut each roll at 2 cm (³/₄ inch) intervals. When cold, store in an airtight container.

PREPARATION TIME: 30 MINUTES +   COOKING TIME: 1 HOUR 10 MINUTES

LIGHT FRUIT BREAD

125 g (4$\frac{1}{2}$ oz/1 cup) raisins
1 tablespoon sherry
1 tablespoon grated orange zest
2 teaspoons dried yeast
250 ml (9 fl oz/1 cup) milk, warmed
55 g (2 oz/$\frac{1}{4}$ cup) caster (superfine) sugar
375 g (13 oz/3 cups) white strong flour
30 g (1 oz) butter, cubed

GLAZE
1 egg yolk
2 tablespoons pouring (whipping) cream

SERVES 8–10

Combine the raisins, sherry and zest in a small bowl and set aside.

Place the yeast, milk and 1 teaspoon of the sugar in a small bowl and mix well. Leave in a warm, draught-free place for 10 minutes, or until bubbles appear on the surface. The mixture should be frothy and slightly increased in volume. If your yeast doesn't foam, it is dead, so you will have to discard it and start again.

Place 340 g (11$\frac{3}{4}$ oz/2$\frac{3}{4}$ cups) of the strong flour and $\frac{1}{2}$ teaspoon salt in a large bowl. Rub in the butter and remaining sugar with your fingertips. Make a well in the centre, add the yeast mixture and mix to a soft dough. Turn out onto a floured surface and knead for 10 minutes, or until smooth and elastic, incorporating the remaining flour as necessary.

Place the dough in an oiled bowl and brush with oil. Cover with plastic wrap or a damp tea towel (dish towel) and leave for 1 hour, or until well risen. Punch down, knead for 2 minutes, then roll to a rectangle, 20 x 40 cm (8 x 16 inches). Scatter with the raisins and roll up firmly from the long end.

Grease a loaf (bar) tin with a base measuring 8 x 21 cm (3$\frac{1}{4}$ x 8$\frac{1}{4}$ inches) and line the base with baking paper. Place the dough in the tin, cover with plastic wrap or a damp tea towel and leave for 30 minutes, or until well risen. Preheat the oven to 180°C (350°F/Gas 4).

To make the glaze, combine the egg yolk and cream and brush a little over the loaf. Bake for 30 minutes, or until cooked and golden. Glaze again, bake for 5 minutes then glaze again. Cool on a wire rack.

PREPARATION TIME: 25 MINUTES +   COOKING TIME: 35 MINUTES

PRINCESS FINGERS

125 g (4^1/2 oz) unsalted butter, cubed and softened
80 g (2^3/4 oz/^{1}/3 cup) caster (superfine) sugar
1 teaspoon natural vanilla extract
2 egg yolks
250 g (9 oz/2 cups) plain (all-purpose) flour
1 teaspoon baking powder
1 tablespoon milk
160 g (5^3/4 oz/^{1}/2 cup) raspberry jam
40 g (1^1/2 oz/^{1}/3 cup) chopped walnuts
80 g (2^3/4 oz/^{1}/3 cup) chopped red glacé cherries
2 egg whites
1 tablespoon grated orange zest
115 g (4 oz/^{1}/2 cup) caster (superfine) sugar, extra
45 g (1^3/4 oz/^{1}/2 cup) desiccated coconut
30 g (1 oz/1 cup) puffed rice cereal

MAKES 24

Preheat the oven to 180°C (350°F/Gas 4). Lightly grease a 20 x 30 cm (8 x 12 inch) shallow tin and line with baking paper, leaving the paper hanging over on the two long sides. Cream the butter, sugar and vanilla using electric beaters until light and fluffy. Add the egg yolks, one at a time, beating thoroughly after each addition.

Sift the flour and baking powder into a bowl, then fold into the creamed mixture with a metal spoon. Fold in the milk, then press evenly and firmly into the tin. Spread the jam over the surface and sprinkle with the chopped walnuts and cherries.

Beat the egg whites in a small, dry bowl until stiff peaks form. Fold in the orange zest and extra sugar with a metal spoon, then fold in the coconut and puffed rice cereal. Spread over the slice with a metal spatula.

Bake for 30–35 minutes, or until firm and golden brown. Cool the slice in the tin. Lift out the slice, using the paper as handles, and cut into fingers. This slice can be kept for up to 4 days in an airtight container.

PREPARATION TIME: 35 MINUTES   COOKING TIME: 35 MINUTES

AFGHANS

150 g (5^1/2 oz) unsalted butter, softened
60 g (2^1/4 oz/^{1}/3 cup) soft brown sugar
1 egg, lightly beaten
1 teaspoon natural vanilla extract
125 g (4^1/2 oz/1 cup) plain (all-purpose) flour
2 tablespoons unsweetened cocoa powder
30 g (1 oz/^{1}/3 cup) desiccated coconut
75 g (2^3/4 oz/1^1/2 cups) lightly crushed cornflakes
90 g (3^1/4 oz/^{1}/2 cup) dark chocolate chips

MAKES 25

Preheat the oven to 180°C (350°F/Gas 4). Line two baking trays with baking paper. Cream the butter and sugar in a large bowl using electric beaters until light and fluffy. Add the egg and vanilla and beat thoroughly.

Add the sifted flour and cocoa to the bowl with the coconut and cornflakes. Stir with a metal spoon until the ingredients are just combined. Put level tablespoons of mixture on the trays, allowing room for spreading. Bake for 20 minutes or until lightly browned, then leave on the tray to cool.

Place the chocolate chips in a small heatproof bowl. Bring a saucepan of water to the boil, then remove from the heat. Sit the bowl over the pan, making sure the base of the bowl does not touch the water. Stir until the chocolate has melted and the mixture is smooth. Spread the biscuits thickly with chocolate and allow to set.

PREPARATION TIME: 20 MINUTES +   COOKING TIME: 25 MINUTES

CHELSEA BUNS

2 teaspoons dried yeast
1 teaspoon sugar
310 g (11 oz/2^1/$_2$ cups) plain (all-purpose) flour, sifted
125 ml (4 fl oz/^{1}/$_2$ cup) milk, warmed
185 g (6^1/$_2$ oz) unsalted butter, cubed
1 tablespoon sugar, extra
2 teaspoons grated lemon zest
1 teaspoon ground mixed (pumpkin pie) spice
1 egg, lightly beaten
45 g (1^3/$_4$ oz/^{1}/$_4$ cup) soft brown sugar
185 g (6^1/$_2$ oz/1 cup) mixed dried fruit
1 tablespoon milk, extra, to glaze
2 tablespoons sugar, extra, to glaze

GLACÉ ICING
60 g (2^1/$_4$ oz/^{1}/$_2$ cup) icing (confectioners') sugar
1–2 tablespoons milk

MAKES 8

Combine the yeast, sugar and 1 tablespoon of the flour in a small bowl. Add the milk and mix until smooth. Leave in a warm, draught-free place for 10 minutes, or until bubbles appear on the surface. The mixture should be frothy and slightly increased in volume. If your yeast doesn't foam, it is dead, so you will have to discard it and start again. Place the remaining flour in a large bowl and rub in 125 g (4^1/$_2$ oz) of the butter with your fingertips. Stir in the extra sugar, lemon zest and half the mixed spice. Make a well in the centre, add the yeast mixture and egg and mix. Gather together and turn out onto a lightly floured surface.

Knead for 2 minutes, or until smooth, then shape into a ball. Place in a large, lightly oiled bowl, cover with plastic wrap and set aside in a warm place for 1 hour, or until well risen. Punch down and knead for 2 minutes, or until smooth.

Preheat the oven to 210°C (415°F/Gas 6–7). Lightly grease a baking tray. Beat the remaining butter with the brown sugar in a small bowl using electric beaters until light and creamy. Roll the dough out to a 25 x 40 cm (10 x 16 inch) rectangle. Spread the butter mixture all over the dough to within 2 cm (^{3}/$_4$ inch) of the edge of one of the longer sides. Spread with the combined fruit and remaining spice. Roll the dough from the long side, firmly and evenly, to enclose the fruit. Use a sharp knife to cut the roll into eight slices about 5 cm (2 inch) wide. Arrange the slices, close together and with the seams inwards, on the tray. Flatten slightly.

Set aside, covered with plastic wrap, in a warm place for 30 minutes, or until well risen. Bake for 20 minutes, or until brown and cooked. When almost ready, stir the extra milk and sugar for glazing in a small saucepan over low heat until the sugar dissolves and the mixture is almost boiling. Brush over the hot buns. Cool.

To make the icing (frosting), mix the icing sugar and milk, stir until smooth, then drizzle over the buns.

PREPARATION TIME: 30 MINUTES +   COOKING TIME: 25 MINUTES

SWISS ROLL

90 g (3¼ oz/¾ cup) self-raising flour
3 eggs, lightly beaten
170 g (6 oz/¾ cup) caster (superfine) sugar
160 g (5¾ oz/½ cup) strawberry jam, beaten
icing (confectioners') sugar, to sprinkle

SERVES 10

Preheat the oven to 190°C (375°F/Gas 5). Lightly grease a shallow 2 x 25 x 30 cm (¾ x 10 x 12 inch) Swiss roll tin (jelly roll tin) and line the base with baking paper, extending over the two long sides. Sift the flour three times onto baking paper.

Beat the eggs using electric beaters in a small bowl for 5 minutes, or until thick and pale. Add 115 g (4 oz/½ cup) of the sugar gradually, beating constantly until the mixture is pale and glossy. Transfer to a large bowl. Using a metal spoon, fold in the flour quickly and lightly. Spread into the tin and smooth the surface. Bake for 10–12 minutes, or until lightly golden and springy to touch. Meanwhile, place a clean tea towel (dish towel) on a work surface, cover with baking paper and lightly sprinkle with the remaining caster sugar. When the cake is cooked, turn it out immediately onto the sugar.

Using the tea towel as a guide, carefully roll the cake up from the short side, rolling the paper inside the roll. Stand the rolled cake on a wire rack for 5 minutes, then carefully unroll and allow the cake to cool to room temperature. Spread with the jam and re-roll. Trim the ends with a knife. Sprinkle with icing sugar.

PREPARATION TIME: 25 MINUTES   COOKING TIME: 12 MINUTES

DATE AND WALNUT ROLLS

90 g (3¼ oz/¾ cup) self-raising flour
90 g (3¼ oz/¾ cup) plain (all-purpose) flour
½ teaspoon bicarbonate of soda (baking soda)
1 teaspoon ground mixed (pumpkin pie) spice
125 g (4½ oz/1 cup) chopped walnuts
100 g (3½ oz) unsalted butter, chopped
140 g (5 oz/¾ cup) soft brown sugar
240 g (8½ oz/1½ cups) chopped stoned dates
1 egg, lightly beaten

SERVES 12

Preheat the oven to 180°C (350°F/Gas 4). Lightly grease two 8 x 17 cm (3¼ x 6½ inch) nut-roll tins and their lids. Sift the flours, bicarbonate of soda and spice into a bowl, then stir in the walnuts. Make a well in the centre.

Combine the butter, sugar, dates and 125 ml (4½ fl oz/½ cup) water in a saucepan. Stir constantly over low heat until the butter has melted and the sugar has dissolved. Remove from the heat and set aside to cool slightly. Add the butter mixture and egg to the flour and stir well.

Spoon the mixture evenly into the prepared tins. Bake, with the tins upright on a baking tray, for 1 hour, or until a skewer inserted into the centre of the loaves comes out clean. Leave in the tins, with the lids on, for 10 minutes before turning out onto a wire rack to cool. Serve in slices. Delicious buttered.

PREPARATION TIME: 25 MINUTES   COOKING TIME: 1 HOUR 10 MINUTES

SWEDISH TEA RING

2 teaspoons dried yeast

170 ml (5$\frac{1}{2}$ fl oz/$\frac{2}{3}$ cup) milk

60 g (2$\frac{1}{4}$ oz) unsalted butter, softened

2 tablespoons caster (superfine) sugar

375 g (13 oz/3 cups) plain (all-purpose) flour

1 egg, lightly beaten

1 egg yolk, extra

FILLING

30 g (1 oz) unsalted butter

1 tablespoon caster (superfine) sugar

100 g (3$\frac{1}{2}$ oz) roughly ground blanched almonds

95 g (3$\frac{1}{2}$ oz/$\frac{1}{2}$ cup) mixed dried fruit

105 g (3$\frac{3}{4}$ oz/$\frac{1}{2}$ cup) glacé cherries, halved

ICING

125 g (4$\frac{1}{2}$ oz/1 cup) icing (confectioners') sugar

1–2 tablespoons milk

2 drops natural almond extract

SERVES 10–12

Lightly grease a baking tray or line with baking paper. Dissolve the yeast in 2 tablespoons warm water in a bowl. Leave in a warm, draught-free place for 10 minutes, or until bubbles appear on the surface. The mixture should be frothy and slightly increased in volume. If your yeast doesn't foam, it is dead, so you will have to discard it and start again. Heat the milk, butter, sugar and $\frac{1}{2}$ teaspoon salt in a saucepan until just warmed.

Sift 250 g (9 oz/2 cups) of the flour into a large bowl. Add the yeast and milk mixtures and beaten egg and mix to a smooth batter. Add enough of the remaining flour to make a soft dough. Turn out onto a lightly floured surface and knead for 10 minutes, or until the dough is smooth and elastic. Place the dough in a large, lightly oiled bowl and brush the dough with oil. Cover with plastic wrap or a damp tea towel (dish towel) and leave in a warm place for 1 hour, or until well risen.

Meanwhile, to make the filling, cream the butter and sugar using electric beaters until light and fluffy, then mix in the almonds, mixed dried fruit and cherries.

Punch the dough down and knead for 1 minute. Roll the dough to a 25 x 45 cm (10 x 17$\frac{3}{4}$ inch) rectangle. Spread the filling over the dough, leaving a 2 cm ($\frac{3}{4}$ inch) border. Roll up and form into a ring with the seam underneath. Mix the egg yolk with 1 tablespoon water and use a little to seal the ends together. Place on the tray. Snip with scissors from the outside edge at 4 cm (1$\frac{1}{2}$ inch) intervals. Cut towards the centre of the ring, about two-thirds of the way in. Turn the cut pieces on the side and flatten slightly, giving it a petal-like appearance. Cover with plastic wrap and leave in a warm place for 45 minutes, or until well risen.

Preheat the oven to 180°C (350°F/Gas 4). Brush the tea ring with some of the egg yolk and water and bake for 20–25 minutes, or until firm and golden. Cover with foil if the tea cake is browning too much. Remove and cool.

To make the icing (frosting), combine the ingredients until smooth. Drizzle over the tea ring.

PREPARATION TIME: 1 HOUR +   COOKING TIME: 30 MINUTES

APPLE AND SPICE TEACAKE

180 g (6¹/₂ oz) unsalted butter, softened
95 g (3¹/₂ oz/¹/₂ cup) soft brown sugar
2 teaspoons finely grated lemon zest
3 eggs, lightly beaten
125 g (4¹/₂ oz/1 cup) self-raising flour
75 g (2³/₄ oz/¹/₂ cup) wholemeal (whole-wheat) flour
¹/₂ teaspoon ground cinnamon
125 ml (4 fl oz/¹/₂ cup) milk
400 g (14 oz) tinned pie apple
¹/₄ teaspoon ground mixed (pumpkin pie) spice
1 tablespoon soft brown sugar, extra
25 g (1 oz/¹/₄ cup) flaked almonds

SERVES 8

Preheat the oven to 180°C (350°F/Gas 4). Grease the base and side of a 20 cm (8 inch) spring-form cake tin, and line the base with baking paper.

Cream the butter and sugar in a small bowl using electric beaters until light and fluffy. Beat in the lemon zest. Add the egg gradually, beating thoroughly after each addition. Transfer the mixture to a large bowl. Using a metal spoon, fold in the sifted flours and cinnamon alternately with the milk. Stir until the mixture is just combined and almost smooth.

Spoon half the mixture into the tin, top with three-quarters of the pie apple, then the remaining cake mixture. Press the remaining pie apple around the edge of the top. Combine the mixed spice, extra sugar and flaked almonds and sprinkle over the cake.

Bake for 1 hour, or until a skewer inserted into the centre of the cake comes out clean. Leave in the tin for 15 minutes before turning out onto a wire rack to cool.

PREPARATION TIME: 30 MINUTES   COOKING TIME: 1 HOUR

CINNAMON TEACAKE

60 g (2¹/₄ oz) unsalted butter, softened
125 g (4¹/₂ oz) caster (superfine) sugar
1 egg, lightly beaten
1 teaspoon natural vanilla extract
90 g (3¹/₄ oz/³/₄ cup) self-raising flour
30 g (1 oz/¹/₄ cup) plain (all-purpose) flour
125 ml (4 fl oz/¹/₂ cup) milk

TOPPING
20 g (³/₄ oz) unsalted butter, melted
1 tablespoon caster (superfine) sugar
1 teaspoon ground cinnamon

SERVES 8

Preheat the oven to 180°C (350°F/Gas 4). Grease a 20 cm (8 inch) round shallow cake tin and line the base with baking paper.

Cream the butter and sugar in a small bowl using electric beaters until light and fluffy. Add the egg gradually, beating thoroughly after each addition. Beat in the vanilla, then transfer to a large bowl. Using a metal spoon, fold in the sifted flours alternately with the milk. Stir until smooth. Spoon into the tin and bake for 30 minutes, or until a skewer inserted into the centre of the cake comes out clean. Leave in the tin for 5 minutes before turning out onto a wire rack.

To make the topping, brush the warm cake with the butter and sprinkle with the sugar and cinnamon.

PREPARATION TIME: 20 MINUTES   COOKING TIME: 30 MINUTES

CLASSIC SPONGE

75 g (2³/₄ oz) plain (all-purpose) flour
150 g (5¹/₂ oz) self-raising flour
6 eggs
220 g (7³/₄ oz) caster (superfine) sugar
2 tablespoons boiling water
160 g (5³/₄ oz/¹/₂ cup) strawberry jam
250 ml (9 fl oz/1 cup) pouring (whipping) cream
icing (confectioners') sugar, to dust

SERVES 8

Preheat the oven to 180°C (350°F/Gas 4). Lightly grease two 22 cm (8¹/₂ inch) sandwich tins or round cake tins and line the bases with baking paper. Dust the tins with a little flour, shaking off any excess.

Sift the flours together three times onto a sheet of baking paper. Beat the eggs in a large bowl using electric beaters for 7 minutes, or until thick and pale. Gradually add the sugar to the egg, beating thoroughly after each addition. Using a large metal spoon, quickly and gently fold in the sifted flour and boiling water.

Spread the mixture evenly into the tins and bake for 25 minutes, or until the sponges are lightly golden and shrink slightly from the sides of the tins. Leave the sponges in their tins for 5 minutes before turning out onto a wire rack to cool.

Spread jam over one of the sponges. Beat the cream in a small bowl until stiff, then spoon into a piping (icing) bag and pipe rosettes over the jam. Place the other sponge on top. Dust with icing sugar.

PREPARATION TIME: 20 MINUTES +   COOKING TIME: 25 MINUTES

NOTES: The secret to making a perfect sponge lies in the folding technique. A beating action, or using a wooden spoon, will cause loss of volume in the egg mixture and result in a flat, heavy cake.

Unfilled sponges can be frozen for up to 1 month — freeze in separate freezer bags. Thaw at room temperature for about 20 minutes. Once a sponge is filled, it is best served immediately.

ORANGE CAKE

250 g (9 oz/2 cups) self-raising flour
40 g ($1^{1}/_{2}$ oz/$^{1}/_{3}$ cup) custard powder or instant vanilla pudding mix
310 g (11 oz/$1^{1}/_{3}$ cups) caster (superfine) sugar
80 g ($2^{3}/_{4}$ oz) unsalted butter, chopped and softened
3 eggs
2 teaspoons finely grated orange zest
250 ml (9 fl oz/1 cup) orange juice

ORANGE BUTTERCREAM

90 g ($3^{1}/_{4}$ oz/$^{3}/_{4}$ cup) icing (confectioners') sugar
125 g ($4^{1}/_{2}$ oz) unsalted butter, softened
1 tablespoon orange juice
1 teaspoon finely grated orange zest

SERVES 8–10

Preheat the oven to 180°C (350°F/Gas 4). Lightly grease the base and side of a 23 cm (9 inch) round cake tin and line the base with baking paper.

Sift the flour and custard powder into a large bowl and add the sugar, butter, eggs, orange zest and juice. Beat using electric beaters for 4 minutes, or until the mixture is smooth. Spoon the mixture into the tin and smooth the surface. Bake for 50 minutes, or until a skewer inserted into the centre of the cake comes out clean. Leave the cake in the tin for 5 minutes before turning out onto a wire rack to cool completely.

To make the buttercream, beat all the ingredients in a small bowl using electric beaters until smooth and creamy. Spread evenly over the cake.

PREPARATION TIME: 15 MINUTES + COOKING TIME: 50 MINUTES

NOTE: To make a cream cheese topping for this cake, mix 125 g ($4^{1}/_{2}$ oz/$^{1}/_{2}$ cup) softened cream cheese with 2 tablespoons icing sugar until well blended, then spread over the top of the cake.

POUND CAKE

375 g (13 oz) unsalted butter, softened
345 g (12 oz/$1^{1}/_{2}$ cups) caster (superfine) sugar
1 teaspoon natural vanilla extract
6 eggs, lightly beaten
375 g (13 oz/3 cups) plain (all-purpose) flour, sifted
1 teaspoon baking powder
60 ml (2 fl oz/$^{1}/_{4}$ cup) milk
icing (confectioners') sugar, to dust

SERVES 8

Preheat the oven to 180°C (350°F/Gas 4). Lightly grease the base and side of a 22 cm ($8^{1}/_{2}$ inch) round cake tin and line the base with baking paper.

Cream the butter and sugar in a small bowl using electric beaters until the mixture is light and fluffy. Beat in the vanilla, then add the eggs gradually, beating thoroughly after each addition. Transfer to a large bowl. Using a metal spoon, fold in the sifted flour and baking powder alternately with the milk. Stir until the mixture is just combined and almost smooth.

Spoon the mixture into the tin and smooth the surface. Bake for 1 hour, or until a skewer inserted into the centre of the cake comes out clean. Leave in the tin for 10 minutes before turning out onto a wire rack to cool. Lightly dust the top with icing sugar just before serving.

PREPARATION TIME: 25 MINUTES   COOKING TIME: 1 HOUR

ORANGE POPPY SEED CAKE

185 g (6½ oz/1½ cups) self-raising flour
35 g (1¼ oz/⅓ cup) ground almonds
40 g (1½ oz/¼ cup) poppy seeds
185 g (6½ oz) unsalted butter
145 g (5½ oz/⅔ cup) caster (superfine) sugar
80 g (2¾ oz/¼ cup) apricot jam or marmalade
2-3 teaspoons finely grated orange zest
80 ml (2½ fl oz/⅓ cup) orange juice
3 eggs, lightly beaten
orange zest, to decorate (optional)

CREAM CHEESE ICING
100 g (3½ oz) unsalted butter, softened
100 g (3½ oz) cream cheese, softened
125 g (4½ oz/1 cup) icing (confectioners') sugar, sifted
1 teaspoon lemon juice or natural vanilla extract

SERVES 8–10

Preheat the oven to 180°C (350°F/Gas 4). Lightly grease a deep 20 cm (8 inch) round cake tin and line with baking paper. Sift the flour into a bowl and add the almonds and poppy seeds. Make a well in the centre.

Place the butter, sugar, jam, orange zest and juice in a saucepan. Stir over low heat until the butter has melted and the mixture is smooth. Gradually add the butter mixture to the dry ingredients, stirring with a whisk until smooth. Add the egg and whisk until combined. Pour into the tin and bake for 50-60 minutes, or until a skewer inserted into the centre of the cake comes out clean. Leave in the tin for 15 minutes before turning onto a wire rack to cool.

To make the icing (frosting), beat the butter and cream cheese until smooth. Gradually add the icing sugar and lemon juice or natural vanilla extract and beat until thick and creamy. Spread the icing over the cooled cake. Decorate with strips of orange zest, if desired.

PREPARATION TIME: 30 MINUTES +   COOKING TIME: 1 HOUR

CARROT CAKE

125 g (4½ oz/1 cup) self-raising flour
125 g (4½ oz/1 cup) plain (all-purpose) flour
2 teaspoons ground cinnamon
1 teaspoon ground ginger
½ teaspoon freshly grated nutmeg
1 teaspoon bicarbonate of soda
(baking soda)
250 ml (9 fl oz/1 cup) oil
185 g (6½ oz/1 cup) soft brown sugar
4 eggs
175 g (6 oz/½ cup) golden syrup or dark
corn syrup
390 g (13¾ oz/2½ cups) grated carrot
60 g (2¼ oz/½ cup) chopped pecans
freshly grated nutmeg, extra, to sprinkle

LEMON ICING
175 g (6 oz) cream cheese, softened
60 g (2¼ oz) unsalted butter, softened
185 g (6½ oz/1½ cups) icing
(confectioners') sugar
1 teaspoon natural vanilla extract
1–2 teaspoons lemon juice

SERVES 8–10

Preheat the oven to 160°C (315°F/Gas 2–3). Lightly grease a 23 cm (9 inch) round cake tin and line the base and side with baking paper. Sift the flours, cinnamon, ginger, nutmeg and bicarbonate of soda into a large bowl and make a well in the centre.

Whisk together the oil, sugar, eggs and golden syrup until combined. Add this mixture to the well in the flour and gradually stir with a metal spoon until smooth. Stir in the carrot and nuts, then spoon into the tin and smooth the surface. Bake for 1½ hours, or until a skewer inserted into the centre of the cake comes out clean. Leave the cake in the tin for at least 15 minutes before turning out onto a wire rack to cool completely.

To make the icing (frosting), beat the cream cheese and butter using electric beaters until smooth. Gradually add the icing sugar alternately with the vanilla and lemon juice, beating until light and creamy. Spread the icing over the cake using a flat-bladed knife. Sprinkle with freshly grated nutmeg.

PREPARATION TIME: 40 MINUTES +   COOKING TIME: 1 HOUR 30 MINUTES

MADEIRA CAKE

185 g (6½ oz) unsalted butter, softened
170 g (6 oz/¾ cup) caster (superfine)
sugar
3 eggs, lightly beaten
2 teaspoons finely grated orange or
lemon zest
155 g (5½ oz/1¼ cups) self-raising flour,
sifted
125 g (4½ oz/1 cup) plain (all-purpose)
flour
2 tablespoons milk

SERVES 8

Preheat the oven to 160°C (315°F/Gas 2–3). Lightly grease a loaf (bar) tin with a base measuring 7 x 10 x 20 cm (2¾ x 4 x 8 inches) and line the base and sides with baking paper.

Cream the butter and sugar in a small bowl using electric beaters until light and fluffy. Add the egg gradually, beating thoroughly after each addition. Add the orange zest and beat until combined. Transfer to a large bowl. Using a metal spoon, fold in the flours and milk. Stir until smooth. Spoon into the tin and smooth the surface. Bake for 50 minutes, or until a skewer inserted into the centre of the cake comes out clean. Cool the cake in the tin for 10 minutes before turning out onto a wire rack to cool completely.

PREPARATION TIME: 20 MINUTES   COOKING TIME: 50 MINUTES

NEW YORK CHEESECAKE

60 g (2¼ oz/½ cup) self-raising flour
125 g (4½ oz/1 cup) plain (all-purpose) flour
55 g (2 oz/¼ cup) caster (superfine) sugar
1 teaspoon grated lemon zest
80 g (2¾ oz) unsalted butter, chopped
1 egg
375 ml (13 fl oz/1½ cups) pouring (whipping) cream, to serve

FILLING
750 g (1 lb 10 oz/3 cups) cream cheese, softened
230 g (8½ oz/1 cup) caster (superfine) sugar
30 g (1 oz/¼ cup) plain (all-purpose) flour
2 teaspoons grated orange zest
2 teaspoons grated lemon zest
4 eggs
170 ml (5½ fl oz/⅔ cup) pouring (whipping) cream

CANDIED ZEST
finely shredded zest of 3 limes, 3 lemons and 3 oranges
230 g (8½ oz/1 cup) caster (superfine) sugar

SERVES 10–12

Preheat the oven to 210°C (415°F/Gas 6-7). Lightly grease a 23 cm (9 inch) spring-form cake tin.

To make the pastry, combine the flours, sugar, lemon zest and butter for about 30 seconds in a food processor, until crumbly. Add the egg and process briefly until the mixture just comes together. Turn out onto a lightly floured surface and gather together into a ball. Refrigerate in plastic wrap for about 20 minutes, or until the mixture is firm.

Roll the dough between two sheets of baking paper until large enough to fit the base and side of the tin. Ease into the tin and trim the edges. Cover the pastry with baking paper, then baking beads or uncooked rice. Bake for 10 minutes, then remove the baking paper and rice. Flatten the pastry lightly with the back of a spoon and bake for another 5 minutes. Set aside to cool.

To make the filling, reduce the oven to 150°C (300°F/Gas 2). Beat the cream cheese, sugar, flour and orange and lemon zest until smooth. Add the eggs, one at a time, beating after each addition. Beat in the cream, pour over the pastry and bake for 1½ hours, or until almost set. Turn off the oven and leave to cool with the door ajar. When cool, refrigerate.

To make the candied zest, place a little water in a saucepan with the lime, lemon and orange zest, bring to the boil and simmer for 1 minute. Drain the zest and repeat with fresh water. This will get rid of any bitterness in the zest and syrup. Put the sugar in a saucepan with 60 ml (2 fl oz/¼ cup) water and stir over low heat until dissolved. Add the zest, bring to the boil, reduce the heat and simmer for 5–6 minutes, or until the zest looks translucent. Allow to cool, drain the zest and place on baking paper to dry (you can save the syrup to serve with the cheesecake). Whip the cream, spoon over the cold cheesecake and top with candied zest.

PREPARATION TIME: 1 HOUR +   COOKING TIME: 1 HOUR 50 MINUTES

NOTE: To make the cheesecake easier to cut, heap the zest in mounds, then cut between the mounds of zest.

PINEAPPLE UPSIDE-DOWN CAKE

90 g (3¼ oz) unsalted butter, melted

95 g (3½ oz/½ cup) soft brown sugar

440 g (15½ oz) tinned pineapple rings in natural juice

6 red glacé cherries

125 g (4½ oz) unsalted butter, extra, softened

170 g (6 oz/¾ cup) caster (superfine) sugar

2 eggs, lightly beaten

1 teaspoon natural vanilla extract

185 g (6½ oz/1½ cups) self-raising flour

60 g (2¼ oz/½ cup) plain (all-purpose) flour

30 g (1 oz/⅓ cup) desiccated coconut

SERVES 8

Preheat the oven to 180°C (350°F/Gas 4). Pour the melted butter into a 20 cm (8 inch) round tin, brushing some of it up the side, but leaving most on the base. Sprinkle the brown sugar over the base. Drain the pineapple, reserving 125 ml (4 fl oz/½ cup) of the juice. Arrange the pineapple rings over the base of the tin (five on the outside and one in the centre) and put a cherry in the centre of each ring.

Cream the extra butter and sugar in a small bowl using electric beaters until light and fluffy. Add the egg gradually, beating thoroughly after each addition. Add the vanilla and beat until combined. Transfer to a large bowl. Using a metal spoon, fold in the sifted flours, then add the coconut and reserved pineapple juice. Stir until the mixture is just combined and almost smooth. Spoon the mixture into the tin over the pineapple rings and smooth the surface. Indent the centre slightly with the back of a spoon to ensure the cake has a reasonably flat base. Bake for 50-60 minutes, or until a skewer inserted into the centre of the cake comes out clean. Leave the cake in the tin for 10 minutes before turning out onto a wire rack to cool.

PREPARATION TIME: 30 MINUTES   COOKING TIME: 1 HOUR

SEED CAKE

125 g (4½ oz) unsalted butter, softened

115 g (4 oz/½ cup) caster (superfine) sugar

3 eggs, lightly beaten

3 teaspoons caraway seeds

155 g (5½ oz/1¼ cups) self-raising flour

2 tablespoons milk

icing (confectioners') sugar, to dust (optional)

SERVES 6–8

Preheat the oven to 180°C (350°F/Gas 4). Lightly grease the base and side of an 18 cm (7 inch) round cake tin, and line the base with baking paper. Cream the butter and sugar in a small bowl using electric beaters until light and fluffy. Add the egg gradually, beating thoroughly after each addition.

Transfer the mixture to a large bowl. Using a metal spoon, fold in the caraway seeds and sifted flour alternately with the milk. Stir until the mixture is just combined and almost smooth. Spoon into the tin and smooth the surface. Bake for 50 minutes, or until a skewer inserted into the centre of the cake comes out clean. Leave in the tin for 20 minutes before turning out onto a wire rack to cool completely. Serve plain or dust with sifted icing sugar.

PREPARATION TIME: 20 MINUTES   COOKING TIME: 50 MINUTES

NOTE: This is a traditional English cake made to celebrate the end of the spring crop sowing.

Pineapple upside-down cake

CREAM BUNS

2 teaspoons dried yeast
2 tablespoons sugar
350 ml (12 fl oz) milk, warmed
435 g (15^1/$_2$ oz/3^1/$_2$ cups) plain (all-purpose) flour
60 g (2^1/$_4$ oz) unsalted butter, melted
160 g (5^3/$_4$ oz/^{1}/$_2$ cup) strawberry jam
310 ml (10^3/$_4$ fl oz/1^1/$_4$ cups) pouring (whipping) cream
1 tablespoon icing (confectioners') sugar
2 tablespoons icing (confectioners') sugar, extra, to dust

MAKES 12

Put the yeast, 1 teaspoon of the sugar and the milk in a small bowl. Leave in a warm, draught-free place for 10 minutes, or until bubbles appear on the surface. The mixture should be frothy and slightly increased in volume. If your yeast doesn't foam, it is dead, so you will have to discard it and start again.

Sift the flour into a large bowl, stir in ^{1}/$_2$ teaspoon salt and the remaining sugar. Make a well in the centre and add the milk mixture and butter and mix to a dough, first with a wooden spoon, then with your hands. Turn onto a lightly floured surface and knead for 10 minutes, or until smooth and elastic. Place in a lightly oiled bowl, cover with plastic wrap, and leave in a warm place for 1 hour, or until well risen.

Punch down the dough and turn onto a lightly floured surface, then knead for 2 minutes or until smooth. Divide into 12 pieces. Knead one portion at a time for 30 seconds on a lightly floured surface and then shape into a ball.

Preheat the oven to 210°C (415°F/Gas 6–7). Lightly grease two baking trays, dust lightly with flour and shake off any excess. Place balls of dough, evenly spaced, on the trays. Set aside, covered with plastic wrap, in a warm place for 15 minutes, or until well risen. Bake for 20 minutes or until well browned and cooked. Set aside for 5 minutes before transferring to a wire rack to cool completely. Using a serrated knife, make a slanted cut into the centre of each bun, to a depth of 5 cm (2 inches), from the top towards the base.

Spread jam over the cut base of each bun. Using electric beaters, beat the cream and icing sugar in a small bowl until firm peaks form. Spoon into a piping (icing) bag and pipe the whipped cream into the buns. Dust the tops with the extra icing sugar.

PREPARATION TIME: 40 MINUTES +   COOKING TIME: 20 MINUTES

BOILED FRUIT CAKE

250 g (9 oz) unsalted butter
185 g (6¹/₂ oz/1 cup) soft brown sugar
1 kg (2 lb 4 oz) mixed dried fruit
125 ml (4 fl oz/¹/₂ cup) sweet sherry
¹/₂ teaspoon bicarbonate of soda (baking soda)
185 g (6¹/₂ oz/1¹/₂ cups) self-raising flour
125 g (4¹/₂ oz/1 cup) plain (all-purpose) flour
1 teaspoon ground mixed (pumpkin pie) spice
4 eggs, lightly beaten

SERVES 8–10

Preheat the oven to 180°C (350°F/Gas 4). Lightly grease and line a 22 cm (8¹/₂ inch) round cake tin.

Put the butter, sugar, mixed fruit, sherry and 185 ml (6 fl oz/³/₄ cup) water in a saucepan. Stir over low heat until the butter has melted and the sugar has dissolved. Bring to the boil, reduce the heat and simmer for 10 minutes. Remove from the heat, stir in the bicarbonate of soda and cool.

Sift the flours and spice into a large bowl and make a well in the centre. Add the egg to the fruit, mix well, then pour into the well and mix thoroughly. Pour into the tin and smooth the surface. Wrap the outside of the tin and sit the cake tin on several layers of newspaper in the oven. Bake for 1–1¹/₄ hours, or until a skewer inserted into the centre of the cake comes out clean. Leave in the tin for at least an hour before turning out onto a wire rack. The flavour improves after standing for 3 days.

PREPARATION TIME: 30 MINUTES   COOKING TIME: 1 HOUR 30 MINUTES

NOTE: This cake can be kept for up to 2 months. The cake colour will depend on the fruit. For a dark cake, use raisins, currants and sultanas (golden raisins). For a lighter colour, mix in chopped glacé fruit.

ANGEL FOOD CAKE

125 g (4¹/₂ oz/1 cup) self-raising flour
345 g (12 oz/1¹/₂ cups) caster (superfine) sugar
12 egg whites
1¹/₂ teaspoons cream of tartar
¹/₂ teaspoon natural vanilla extract
¹/₄ teaspoon natural almond extract
icing (confectioners') sugar, to dust
fresh fruit, sliced or chopped, to serve

SERVES 10–12

Preheat the oven to 180°C (350°F/Gas 4). Have an ungreased angel food tin ready. Sift the flour and 170 g (6 oz/³/₄ cup) of the sugar together four times. Using electric beaters, beat the egg whites with the cream of tartar and ¹/₄ teaspoon salt until stiff peaks form. Beat in the remaining sugar, 1 tablespoon at a time. Fold in the vanilla and almond extracts. Sift one-quarter of the flour and sugar mixture onto the egg white and, using a spatula, gradually fold in. Repeat with the remaining flour and sugar.

Spoon the mixture into the tin and bake for 35–40 minutes, or until puffed and golden and a skewer inserted into the centre of the cake comes out clean. Turn upside-down on a wire rack and leave in the tin until cool. Gently shake to remove the cake. Lightly dust with icing sugar and serve with fruit.

PREPARATION TIME: 30 MINUTES   COOKING TIME: 40 MINUTES

Boiled fruit cake

CHOCOLATE ÉCLAIRS

125 g (4½ oz) unsalted butter
125 g (4½ oz/1 cup) plain (all-purpose) flour, sifted
4 eggs, lightly beaten
300 ml (10½ fl oz) whipped cream
150 g (5½ oz) dark chocolate, chopped

MAKES 18

Preheat the oven to 210°C (415°F/Gas 6–7). Grease two baking trays. Combine the butter and 250 ml (9 fl oz/1 cup) water in a large heavy-based saucepan. Stir over medium heat until the butter melts. Increase the heat, bring to the boil, then remove from the heat.

Add the flour to the saucepan all at once and quickly beat into the water with a wooden spoon. Return to the heat and continue beating until the mixture leaves the side of the pan and forms a ball. Transfer to a large bowl and cool slightly. Beat the mixture to release any remaining heat. Add the egg gradually, 3 teaspoons at a time. Beat thoroughly after each addition until all the egg has been added and the mixture is glossy — a wooden spoon should stand upright in the mixture. If it is too runny, the egg has been added too quickly. If this happens, beat for several more minutes, or until thickened.

Spoon the mixture into a piping (icing) bag fitted with a 1.5 cm (5/8 inch) plain nozzle. Sprinkle the baking trays lightly with water. Pipe 15 cm (6 inch) lengths onto the trays, leaving room for expansion. Bake for 10–15 minutes. Reduce the heat to 180°C (350°F/Gas 4). Bake for 15 minutes, or until golden and firm. Cool on a wire rack. Split each éclair, removing any uncooked dough. Fill the puffs with cream.

Put the chocolate in a heatproof bowl. Bring a saucepan of water to the boil and remove the pan from the heat. Sit the bowl over the pan, making sure the base of the bowl does not touch the water. Allow to stand, stirring occasionally, until the chocolate has melted. Spread over the tops of the éclairs.

PREPARATION TIME: 30 MINUTES   COOKING TIME: 40 MINUTES

BAKEWELL TART

125 g (4¹/2 oz/1 cup) plain (all-purpose) flour
90 g (3¹/4 oz) unsalted butter, chilled and cubed
2 teaspoons caster (superfine) sugar
2 tablespoons iced water

FILLING
90 g (3¹/4 oz) unsalted butter
80 g (2³/4 oz/¹/3 cup) caster (superfine) sugar
2 eggs, lightly beaten
3 drops natural almond extract
70 g (2¹/2 oz/²/3 cup) ground almonds
40 g (1¹/2 oz/¹/3 cup) self-raising flour, sifted
160 g (5³/4 oz/¹/2 cup) raspberry jam
icing (confectioners') sugar, to dust

SERVES 6

Preheat the oven to 180°C (350°F/Gas 4). Lightly grease a 20 cm (8 inch) round, loose-based, fluted flan (tart) tin. Sift the flour into a large bowl and rub in the butter, using your fingertips, until the mixture resembles fine breadcrumbs. Stir in the sugar. Make a well in the centre, then add almost all the water and mix with a flat-bladed knife, using a cutting action, until the mixture comes together in beads, adding more water if the dough is too dry. Gently gather the dough together and roll out between two sheets of baking paper to cover the base and side of the tin. Line the tin with the pastry, trim the edges and refrigerate for 20 minutes. Line the pastry with baking paper and pour in some baking beads or uncooked rice. Bake for 10 minutes, remove the paper and beads, then bake the pastry for another 7 minutes, or until golden. Set aside to cool.

Beat the butter and sugar in a small bowl using electric beaters until light and creamy. Add the egg gradually, beating thoroughly after each addition. Add the almond extract and beat until combined. Transfer to a large bowl and fold in the almonds and flour with a metal spoon. Spread the jam over the pastry, then spoon the almond mixture on top and smooth the surface. Bake for 35 minutes, or until risen and golden. Dust with icing sugar.

PREPARATION TIME: 25 MINUTES +   COOKING TIME: 55 MINUTES

GENOISE SPONGE

290 g (10¹/4 oz/2¹/3 cups) plain (all-purpose) flour
8 eggs
220 g (7³/4 oz) caster (superfine) sugar
100 g (3¹/2 oz) unsalted butter, melted and cooled
icing (confectioners') sugar, sifted, to dust

SERVES 10–12

Preheat the oven to 180°C (350°F/Gas 4). Lightly grease one 25 cm (10 inch) Genoise tin or two shallow 22 cm (8¹/2 inch) round cake tins with melted butter. Line the base with baking paper, then grease the paper. Dust the tin(s) with a little flour, shaking off any excess. Sift the flour three times onto baking paper. Mix the eggs and sugar in a large heatproof bowl. Place the bowl over a pan of simmering water, making sure the base of the bowl does not touch the water, and beat using electric beaters for 8 minutes, or until the mixture is thick and fluffy. Remove from the heat and beat for 3 minutes.

Add the butter and flour. Using a large metal spoon, fold in quickly and lightly until the mixture is just combined. Spread the mixture evenly into the tin. Bake for 25 minutes, or until the sponge is lightly golden and has shrunk slightly from the side of the tin. Leave the cake in the tin for 5 minutes before turning out onto a wire rack to cool. Dust with icing sugar just before serving.

PREPARATION TIME: 25 MINUTES   COOKING TIME: 35 MINUTES

HUMMINGBIRD CAKE

2 ripe bananas, mashed
130 g (4³/₄ oz/¹/₂ cup) drained and crushed tinned pineapple (see NOTE)
285 g (10¹/₄ oz/1¹/₄ cups) caster (superfine) sugar
210 g (7¹/₂ oz/1²/₃ cups) self-raising flour
2 teaspoons ground cinnamon or mixed (pumpkin pie) spice
170 ml (5¹/₂ fl oz/²/₃ cup) oil
60 ml (2 fl oz/¹/₄ cup) pineapple juice
2 eggs

ICING
60 g (2¹/₄ oz) unsalted butter, softened
125 g (4¹/₂ oz/¹/₂ cup) cream cheese, softened
185 g (6¹/₂ oz/1¹/₂ cups) icing (confectioners') sugar
1–2 teaspoons lemon juice

SERVES 8–10

Preheat the oven to 180°C (350°F/Gas 4). Lightly grease a 20 cm (8 inch) square cake tin and line with baking paper.

Place the banana, pineapple and sugar in a large bowl. Add the sifted flour and cinnamon or mixed spice. Stir together with a wooden spoon until well combined.

Whisk together the oil, pineapple juice and eggs. Pour onto the banana mixture and stir until combined and the mixture is smooth.

Spoon into the tin and smooth the surface. Bake for 1 hour, or until a skewer inserted into the centre of the cake comes out clean. Leave in the tin for 15 minutes before turning out onto a wire rack to cool.

To make the icing (frosting), beat the butter and cream cheese using electric beaters until smooth. Gradually add the icing sugar alternately with the lemon juice. Beat until thick and creamy.

Spread the icing thickly over the top of the cooled cake, or thinly over the top and side.

PREPARATION TIME: 30 MINUTES +   COOKING TIME: 1 HOUR

NOTE: If you are unable to buy crushed pineapple, use pineapple rings chopped very finely. Buy the fruit in natural juice rather than syrup and reserve the juice when draining to use in the recipe.

GOLDEN FRUIT CAKE

110 g (3³/₄ oz) chopped glacé pears
240 g (8³/₄ oz/1 cup) chopped glacé apricots
220 g (7³/₄ oz) chopped glacé pineapple
60 g (2¹/₄ oz) chopped mixed peel
95 g (3¹/₂ oz) chopped glacé orange slices
80 g (2³/₄ oz/¹/₂ cup) roughly chopped blanched almonds
185 g (6¹/₂ oz/1¹/₂ cups) plain (all-purpose) flour
60 g (2¹/₄ oz/¹/₂ cup) self-raising flour
250 g (9 oz) unsalted butter, softened
1 tablespoon finely grated orange zest
1 tablespoon finely grated lemon zest
230 g (8¹/₂ oz/1 cup) caster (superfine) sugar
4 eggs
60 ml (2 fl oz/¹/₄ cup) sweet sherry

SERVES 16–20

Preheat the oven to 160°C (315°F/Gas 2–3). Lightly grease a deep 20 cm (8 inch) square tin and line with baking paper.

Combine the fruits and almonds in a bowl and toss with 30 g (1 oz/¹/₄ cup) of the plain flour to help keep the fruits separate. Sift together the remaining flours.

Beat the butter and grated zest in a small bowl using electric beaters, gradually adding the sugar, until light and fluffy. Beat in the eggs, one at a time, beating thoroughly after each addition. Transfer the mixture to a large bowl, stir in the remaining flour alternately with the sherry, then fold in the fruit, nut and flour mixture.

Spread evenly into the tin and wrap paper around the outside of the tin. Sit the cake tin on several layers of newspaper in the oven. Bake for about 1³/₄–2 hours, or until a skewer inserted into the centre of the cake comes out clean. Leave in the tin for 20 minutes before turning out onto a wire rack to cool. Store in an airtight container for up to a month.

PREPARATION TIME: 25 MINUTES COOKING TIME: 2 HOURS

ALMOND TORTE

450 g (1 lb) blanched almonds, lightly toasted
150 g (5¹/₂ oz) unsalted butter, softened
400 g (14 oz/1³/₄ cups) caster (superfine) sugar
6 eggs
150 g (5¹/₂ oz) plain (all-purpose) flour
2 teaspoons grated lemon zest
2 teaspoons lemon juice
icing (confectioners') sugar, to dust

SERVES 8

Preheat the oven to 170°C (325°F/Gas 3). Lightly grease a 24 cm (9¹/₂ inch) spring-form cake tin. Grind the almonds finely in a food processor and set aside.

Using electric beaters, cream the butter and sugar in a bowl until light and creamy. Add the eggs one at a time, beating thoroughly after each addition. Using a large metal spoon, fold in the flour, ground almonds and lemon zest. Stir until just combined and almost smooth.

Pour the batter into the prepared tin and bake for 1 hour 20 minutes, or until a skewer inserted into the centre of the cake comes out clean. Allow to cool for 5 minutes, then brush the top with the lemon juice. Turn out onto a wire rack and allow to cool completely. Dust with icing sugar in a cross pattern, using a stencil if you wish.

PREPARATION TIME: 15 MINUTES +   COOKING TIME: 1 HOUR 20 MINUTES

Golden fruit cake

BLACK FOREST GATEAU

125 g (4¹/₂ oz) unsalted butter
230 g (8¹/₂ oz/1 cup) caster (superfine) sugar
2 eggs, lightly beaten
1 teaspoon natural vanilla extract
40 g (1¹/₂ oz/¹/₃ cup) self-raising flour
125 g (4¹/₂ oz/1 cup) plain (all-purpose) flour
1 teaspoon bicarbonate of soda (baking soda)
60 g (2¹/₄ oz/¹/₂ cup) unsweetened cocoa powder
185 ml (6 fl oz/³/₄ cup) buttermilk

TOPPING
100 g (3¹/₂ oz) dark chocolate
100 g (3¹/₂ oz) milk chocolate
cherries with stalks, to decorate

FILLING
60 ml (2 fl oz/¹/₄ cup) Kirsch
750 ml (26 fl oz/3 cups) whipped cream
425 g (15 oz) tinned pitted morello or black cherries, drained
fresh or maraschino cherries, to decorate

SERVES 8–10

Preheat the oven to 180°C (350°F/Gas 4). Lightly grease a deep, 20 cm (8 inch) round cake tin. Line the base and side with baking paper. Using electric beaters, beat the butter and sugar until light and creamy. Add the egg gradually, beating thoroughly after each addition. Add the vanilla and beat until well combined. Transfer to a large bowl. Using a metal spoon, fold in the sifted flours, bicarbonate of soda and cocoa alternately with the buttermilk. Mix until combined and the mixture is smooth.

Pour the mixture into the tin and smooth the surface. Bake the cake for 50–60 minutes, or until a skewer inserted into the centre of the cake comes out clean. Leave the cake in the tin for 30 minutes before turning out onto a wire rack to cool. When cold, cut horizontally into three layers, using a long serrated knife. The easiest way to do this is to rest the palm of one hand lightly on top of the cake while cutting into it. Turn the cake every few strokes so the knife cuts in evenly all the way around the edge. When you have gone the whole way round, cut through the middle. Remove the first layer so it will be easier to see what you are doing while cutting the next one.

To make the topping, leave the chocolate in a warm place for 10–15 minutes, or until soft but still firm. With a vegetable peeler, and using long strokes, shave curls of chocolate from the side of the block. If the block is too soft, chill it to firm it up.

To assemble, place one cake layer on a serving plate and brush liberally with Kirsch. Spread evenly with one-fifth of the whipped cream. Top with half the cherries. Continue layering with the remaining cake, liqueur, cream and cherries, finishing with the cream on top. Spread the cream evenly on the outside of the cake. Coat the side with chocolate shavings by laying the shavings on a small piece of baking paper and then gently pressing them into the cream. If you use your hands, they will melt, so the paper acts as a barrier. Decorate the top of the cake with more chocolate shavings and fresh or maraschino cherries on stalks.

PREPARATION TIME: 1 HOUR +   COOKING TIME: 60 MINUTES

NOTE: Black Forest gateau is probably one of the most famous cakes in the world. It originated in Swabia, Germany, in the Black Forest region. In Germany, it is known as 'Black Forest Torte'.

KIDS' BITES

CHICKEN STRIPS WITH SWEET AND SOUR SAUCE

60 g (2¼ oz/½ cup) plain (all-purpose) flour
1 tablespoon chicken seasoning salt
4 boneless, skinless chicken breasts, cut into 2 cm (¾ inch) wide strips
2 eggs
150 g (5½ oz/1½ cups) dry breadcrumbs
oil, for pan-frying

SWEET AND SOUR SAUCE
250 ml (9 fl oz/1 cup) pineapple juice
60 ml (2 fl oz/¼ cup) white wine vinegar
2 teaspoons soy sauce
2 tablespoons soft brown sugar
2 tablespoons tomato sauce (ketchup)
1 tablespoon cornflour (cornstarch)

MAKES 35–40

Combine the flour and seasoning salt in a plastic bag and toss with the chicken strips to coat. Remove and shake off any excess. Lightly beat the eggs in a shallow bowl and put the breadcrumbs in a plastic bag.

Working with a few chicken strips at a time, dip into the beaten egg, then toss in the breadcrumbs. Transfer to a baking tray covered with baking paper and refrigerate for about 30 minutes.

Heat 3 cm (1¼ inches) oil in a large frying pan to 180°C (350°F), or until a cube of bread dropped into the oil browns in 15 seconds. Fry the strips in batches for 3–5 minutes, or until golden brown. Drain on crumpled paper towels.

To make the sauce, combine the pineapple juice, vinegar, soy sauce, sugar and tomato sauce in a small saucepan. Stir over low heat until the sugar has dissolved. Blend the cornflour with 1 tablespoon water, add to the pan, then stir constantly until the mixture boils and thickens. Reduce the heat and simmer for 2 minutes. Serve with the chicken strips.

PREPARATION TIME: 30 MINUTES +   COOKING TIME: 30 MINUTES

CHEESE TWISTS

1 sheet frozen puff pastry, thawed
1 egg, lightly beaten
25 g (1 oz/$^1/_4$ cup) finely grated parmesan cheese

MAKES 16

Preheat the oven to 210°C (415°F/Gas 6–7). Lay the thawed puff pastry on a work surface and brush lightly with beaten egg. Cut the pastry into 1.5 cm ($^5/_8$ inch) strips. Holding both ends, twist each strip in opposite directions twice.

Put the strips on a lightly greased baking tray. Sprinkle the parmesan over the flat part of the twists. Bake for 10 minutes, or until puffed and golden.

PREPARATION TIME: 5 MINUTES   COOKING TIME: 10 MINUTES

CHEESE BISCUITS

125 g (4$^1/_2$ oz) butter, chopped
125 g (4$^1/_2$ oz) cheddar cheese, grated
2 tablespoons freshly grated parmesan cheese
125 g (4$^1/_2$ oz/1 cup) plain (all-purpose) flour
2 tablespoons self-raising flour
pinch cayenne pepper
2 teaspoons lemon juice

MAKES 45

Put all the ingredients and a pinch of salt in a food processor. Process for 60 seconds, or until the mixture comes together and forms a ball.

Gently knead the mixture for 2 minutes on a lightly floured surface. Form the dough into a sausage shape about 3 cm (1$^1/_4$ inches) in diameter. Wrap in plastic wrap, then in foil and freeze for 30 minutes. Remove and leave at room temperature for 5 minutes.

Preheat the oven to 180°C (350°F/Gas 4). Line two baking trays with baking paper.

Slice the dough into thin slices, about 3 mm ($^1/_8$ inch) thick, and place on the trays, allowing a little room for spreading. Bake the biscuits for 10 minutes, or until golden. Allow to cool on the trays.

PREPARATION TIME: 10 MINUTES +   COOKING TIME: 10 MINUTES

NOTE: Cheese biscuits are best eaten on the day of baking.

SAUSAGE ROLLS

3 sheets frozen puff pastry, thawed
2 eggs, lightly beaten
750 g (1 lb 10 oz) minced (ground) sausage
1 onion, finely chopped
1 garlic clove, crushed
80 g (2³/₄ oz/1 cup) fresh breadcrumbs
3 tablespoons chopped flat-leaf (Italian) parsley
3 tablespoons chopped thyme
¹/₂ teaspoon ground sage
¹/₂ teaspoon freshly grated nutmeg
¹/₂ teaspoon ground cloves

MAKES 36

Preheat the oven to 200°C (400°F/Gas 6). Lightly grease two baking trays.

Cut the pastry sheets in half and lightly brush the edges with some of the beaten egg.

Mix half the remaining egg with the remaining ingredients and ¹/₂ teaspoon black pepper in a large bowl, then divide into six even portions. Pipe or spoon the filling down the centre of each piece of pastry, then brush the edges with some of the egg. Fold the pastry over the filling, overlapping the edges and placing the join underneath. Brush the rolls with more egg, then cut each into six short pieces.

Cut two small slashes on top of each roll, place on the baking trays and bake for 15 minutes. Reduce the heat to 180°C (350°F/Gas 4) and bake for another 15 minutes, or until puffed and golden.

PREPARATION TIME: 30 MINUTES   COOKING TIME: 30 MINUTES

MEATBALLS

4 slices white bread, crusts removed
150 g (5½ oz) minced (ground) pork
150 g (5½ oz) minced (ground) veal
1 tablespoon chopped flat-leaf
(Italian) parsley
1 tablespoon chopped mint
1 onion, grated
½ teaspoon ground cumin
1 egg
25 g (1 oz/¼ cup) freshly grated kefalotyri
cheese or parmesan cheese
60 g (2¼ oz/½ cup) plain (all-purpose)
flour
olive oil, for pan-frying

MAKES ABOUT 28

Cover the bread with water in a bowl, then squeeze out as much water as possible. Place in a large bowl with the minced pork and veal, parsley, mint, onion, cumin, egg and cheese, then season. Knead the mixture by hand for 2–3 minutes until smooth. Cover and refrigerate for 30 minutes.

Put the flour in a shallow dish. With wet hands, roll level tablespoons of the meatball mixture into balls. Heat the oil over medium heat. Toss the meatballs in the flour. Pan-fry in batches for 3–5 minutes, or until the meatballs are browned and cooked through. Drain on crumpled paper towels. Serve hot.

PREPARATION TIME: 25 MINUTES +   COOKING TIME: 20 MINUTES

MINI CORN DOGS

8 large frankfurts, cut in half crossways
cornflour (cornstarch), to dust
oil, for deep-frying
tomato sauce (ketchup), to serve

BATTER
215 g (7¾ oz/1¾ cups) self-raising flour
35 g (1¼ oz/¼ cup) cornmeal
1 teaspoon chopped chilli or pinch chilli
powder (optional)
1 egg, lightly beaten
1 tablespoon oil

MAKES 16

Soak eight wooden skewers in water for 30 minutes, to prevent them from burning during cooking. Cut the skewers in half and insert one half through each frankfurt, leaving some of the skewer sticking out for a handle. Dust the frankfurts with a little cornflour.

To make the batter, sift the flour into a large bowl, stir in the cornmeal and chilli (if desired) and make a well in the centre. Gradually add the combined egg, oil and 375 ml (13 fl oz/1½ cups) water, whisking to make a smooth, lump-free batter.

Fill a deep-fryer or large heavy-based saucepan one-third full of oil and heat to 180°C (350°F), or until a cube of bread dropped into the oil browns in 15 seconds. Dip the frankfurts into the batter a few at a time, draining off the excess batter. Using tongs, gently lower the frankfurts into the oil. Cook over medium–high heat for 1–2 minutes, or until golden and crisp and heated through. Carefully remove from the oil. Drain on crumpled paper towels and keep warm. Repeat with the remaining frankfurts. Serve with tomato sauce.

PREPARATION TIME: 10 MINUTES   COOKING TIME: 10 MINUTES

CRISPY CHICKEN AND FISH WRAPS WITH SWEET AND SOUR SAUCE

SWEET AND SOUR SAUCE
110 g (3¾ oz/½ cup) sugar
125 ml (4 fl oz/½ cup) white vinegar
1 tablespoon tomato sauce (ketchup)
1 tablespoon cornflour (cornstarch)

FILLING
100 g (3½ oz) boneless, skinless chicken, finely chopped
100 g (3½ oz) skinless firm white fish fillets, finely chopped
½ celery stalk, finely chopped
1 small spring onion (scallion), finely chopped
2 teaspoons light soy sauce

30 won ton wrappers
oil, for deep-frying

MAKES 30

To make the sauce, combine the sugar, vinegar and tomato sauce with 185 ml (6 fl oz/¾ cup) water in a small saucepan. Blend the cornflour with 1 tablespoon water in a small bowl. Add to the saucepan and stir over low heat until the mixture boils and thickens and the sugar has dissolved.

To make the filling, combine all the ingredients with ¼ teaspoon salt. Place 1 teaspoon of mixture onto each won ton wrapper. Brush the edges lightly with water. Fold to form a triangle and dab water onto the left front corner of the triangle. Fold the two bottom corners across, one on top of the other, and press together lightly with your finger.

Fill a deep-fryer or heavy-based saucepan one-third full of oil and heat the oil to 180°C (350°F), or until a cube of bread dropped into the oil browns in 15 seconds. Deep-fry in batches until crisp and golden brown. Shake off the excess oil and drain on crumpled paper towel. Serve with the sauce.

PREPARATION TIME: 30 MINUTES   COOKING TIME: 4 MINUTES PER BATCH

GOLDEN POTATO CHIPS

500 g (1 lb 2 oz) all-purpose potatoes
750 ml (26 fl oz/3 cups) oil

SERVES 4

Cut the potatoes into thick country-style chips or wedges. Heat the oil in a saucepan and cook the potatoes in batches until lightly golden. Drain on paper towels. Repeat with the remaining potatoes.

Just before serving, re-fry the potatoes in batches until crisp and golden. Sprinkle with sea salt and malt vinegar, if desired.

PREPARATION TIME: 10 MINUTES   COOKING TIME: 30 MINUTES

POTATO NOODLE NIBBLES

450 g (1 lb) boiling potatoes, peeled and chopped
40 g (1^1/$_2$ oz) butter, softened
2 tablespoons freshly grated parmesan or pecorino cheese
100 g (3^1/$_2$ oz) besan (chickpea flour)
2 teaspoons ground cumin
2 teaspoons garam masala
1 teaspoon ground coriander
1 teaspoon chilli powder (optional)
1 teaspoon cayenne pepper
1^1/$_2$ teaspoons ground turmeric
oil, for deep-frying

SERVES 6

Boil or steam the potato until tender. Drain and cool for 15–20 minutes, then mash with the butter and cheese. Add the besan, cumin, garam masala, coriander, chilli powder (if desired), cayenne pepper, turmeric and ^{3}/$_4$ teaspoon salt and mix with a wooden spoon until a soft, light dough forms. Turn out and knead lightly 10–12 times, until quite smooth.

Fill a deep-fryer or heavy-based saucepan one-third full of oil and heat the oil to 180°C (350°F). Test the temperature by dropping a small ball of dough into the oil. The oil is ready if the dough rises immediately to the surface.

Using a piping (icing) bag fitted with a 1 cm (^{1}/$_2$ inch) star nozzle, pipe short lengths of dough into the oil, cutting the dough off with a knife. Cook in manageable batches. They will rise to the surface and turn golden quickly. Remove with a slotted spoon and drain on crumpled paper towels. Serve the nibbles within 2 hours of cooking.

PREPARATION TIME: 30 MINUTES +   COOKING TIME: 40 MINUTES

SESAME CHICKEN STICKS

4 boneless, skinless chicken breasts, cut into strips
60 ml (2 fl oz/$1/4$ cup) teriyaki sauce
1 tablespoon chilli sauce (optional)
1 tablespoon plain yoghurt
2 teaspoons curry powder
100 g ($3^1/2$ oz/2 cups) crushed cornflakes
40 g ($1^1/2$ oz/$1/4$ cup) sesame seeds
35 g ($1^1/4$ oz) parmesan cheese, grated

SWEET AND SOUR SAUCE
1 tablespoon cornflour (cornstarch)
125 ml (4 fl oz/$1/2$ cup) white vinegar
115 g (4 oz/$1/2$ cup) caster (superfine) sugar
60 ml (2 fl oz/$1/4$ cup) tomato sauce (ketchup)
1 teaspoon chicken stock (bouillon) powder

MAKES ABOUT 32

Combine the chicken strips in a bowl with the teriyaki sauce, chilli sauce (if desired), yoghurt and curry powder. Mix well, cover and refrigerate overnight.

Preheat the oven to 190°C (375°F/Gas 5). Combine the cornflakes, sesame seeds and parmesan in a shallow dish. Drain the excess marinade from the chicken. Coat each chicken strip in the crumb mixture.

Place the strips in a single layer on a greased baking tray. Bake for 20–25 minutes, or until crisp and golden. Serve hot.

Meanwhile, to make the sauce, blend the cornflour with the vinegar and combine with the remaining ingredients and 250 ml (9 fl oz/1 cup) water in a small saucepan. Stir over medium heat until the mixture boils and thickens. Serve with the chicken strips.

PREPARATION TIME: 25 MINUTES +   COOKING TIME: 25 MINUTES

NOTE: The chicken strips can be frozen in a single layer for 2 months.

CHICKEN AND CORN BITES

185 g (6½ oz/1½ cups) self-raising flour
2 teaspoons chicken stock (bouillon) powder
½ teaspoon chicken seasoning salt
60 g (2¼ oz) butter, chopped
50 g (1¾ oz) corn chips, finely crushed
2 eggs, lightly beaten
chicken seasoning salt, extra, to sprinkle

MAKES 50

Preheat the oven to 180°C (350°F/Gas 4). Line a baking tray with baking paper. Sift the flour, stock powder and seasoning salt into a large bowl and add the butter. Rub into the flour with your fingertips until the mixture resembles fine breadcrumbs. Stir in the corn chips. Make a well in the centre, add the eggs and mix with a flat-bladed knife, using a cutting action until the mixture comes together in beads.

Gently gather the dough together, lift out onto a lightly floured surface and press together into a ball. Roll out to 5 mm (¼ inch) thick. Cut the dough into shapes with a plain or fluted biscuit (cookie) cutter. Place on the tray and sprinkle with chicken salt. Bake for 15 minutes, or until lightly browned. Cool on the tray. Store in an airtight container for up to 2 days.

PREPARATION TIME: 15 MINUTES   COOKING TIME: 15 MINUTES

ALMOND-CRUSTED CHEESE BITES

500 g (1 lb 2 oz) cheddar cheese, grated
250 g (9 oz/1 cup) cold cooked and mashed pumpkin (winter squash)
40 g (1½ oz/⅓ cup) plain (all-purpose) flour
1 garlic clove, crushed
2 tablespoons snipped chives or chopped flat-leaf (Italian) parsley
2 egg whites
250 g (9 oz) flaked almonds, roughly crushed
oil, for deep-frying

MAKES 24

Combine the cheese, pumpkin, flour, garlic and chives in a large bowl. Beat the egg whites in a bowl until stiff, then stir into the pumpkin mixture.

Mould small spoonfuls with your hands to form balls. Roll in the almonds, place on baking trays and refrigerate for 1 hour.

Fill a deep-fryer or heavy-based saucepan one-third full of oil and heat the oil to 180°C (350°F), or until a cube of bread dropped into the oil browns in 15 seconds. Deep-fry the balls in batches until golden brown, then drain on crumpled paper towels.

PREPARATION TIME: 30 MINUTES +   COOKING TIME: 20 MINUTES

FINGER BUNS

500 g (1 lb 2 oz/4 cups) plain (all-purpose) flour
35 g (1¼ oz/⅓ cup) milk powder
1 tablespoon dried yeast
115 g (4 oz/½ cup) caster (superfine) sugar
60 g (2¼ oz/½ cup) sultanas (golden raisins)
60 g (2¼ oz) unsalted butter, melted
1 egg, lightly beaten
1 egg yolk, extra, to glaze

GLACÉ ICING
155 g (5½ oz/1¼ cups) icing (confectioners') sugar
20 g (¾ oz) unsalted butter, melted
pink food colouring

MAKES 12

Mix 375 g (13 oz/3 cups) of the flour with the milk powder, yeast, sugar, sultanas and ½ teaspoon salt in a large bowl. Make a well in the centre. Combine the butter, egg and 250 ml (9 fl oz/1 cup) warm water and add all at once to the flour. Stir for 2 minutes, or until well combined. Add enough of the remaining flour to make a soft dough.

Turn out onto a lightly floured surface. Knead for 10 minutes, or until the dough is smooth and elastic, adding more flour if necessary. Place in a large lightly oiled bowl and brush with oil. Cover with plastic wrap and leave in a warm place for 1 hour, or until well risen.

Lightly grease two large baking trays. Preheat the oven to 180°C (350°F/Gas 4). Punch down the dough and knead for 1 minute. Divide into 12 pieces. Shape each into a 15 cm (6 inch) long oval. Put on the trays 5 cm (2 inches) apart. Cover with plastic wrap and set aside in a warm place for 20–25 minutes, or until well risen.

Mix the extra egg yolk with 1½ teaspoons water and brush over the dough. Bake for 12–15 minutes, or until firm and golden. Transfer to a wire rack to cool.

To make the icing (frosting), stir the icing sugar, 2–3 teaspoons water and the melted butter together in a bowl until smooth. Mix in the food colouring and spread over the tops of the buns. Finger buns are delicious buttered.

PREPARATION TIME: 45 MINUTES +   COOKING TIME: 15 MINUTES

CHOCOLATE-CHIP MUFFINS

310 g (11 oz/2$\frac{1}{2}$ cups) self-raising flour
265 g (9$\frac{1}{2}$ oz/1$\frac{1}{2}$ cups) chocolate chips
95 g (3$\frac{1}{2}$ oz/$\frac{1}{2}$ cup) soft brown sugar
375 ml (13 fl oz/1$\frac{1}{2}$ cups) milk
2 eggs, lightly beaten
1 teaspoon natural vanilla extract
150 g (5$\frac{1}{2}$ oz) unsalted butter, melted and cooled

MAKES 12

Preheat the oven to 200°C (400°F/Gas 6). Lightly grease a 12-hole standard muffin tin, or line the muffin tin with paper cases. Sift the flour into a bowl. Add the chocolate chips and sugar to the bowl and stir through the flour. Make a well in the centre.

Mix together the milk, egg and vanilla. Pour the liquid into the well in the flour and add the cooled butter. Fold the mixture gently with a metal spoon until just combined. Do not overmix — the batter will still be slightly lumpy. Divide the mixture evenly among the holes — fill each hole to about three-quarters full.

Bake the muffins for 20-25 minutes, or until they are golden and a skewer inserted into the centre of a muffin comes out clean. Leave the muffins in the tin for a couple of minutes to cool. Gently loosen each muffin with a flat-bladed knife before turning out onto a wire rack. Serve warm or at room temperature.

PREPARATION TIME: 20 MINUTES   COOKING TIME: 25 MINUTES

BANANA MUFFINS

310 g (11 oz/2$\frac{1}{2}$ cups) self-raising flour
170 g (6 oz/$\frac{3}{4}$ cup) caster (superfine) sugar
$\frac{1}{2}$ teaspoon ground mixed (pumpkin pie) spice
250 ml (9 fl oz/1 cup) milk
2 eggs, lightly beaten
1 teaspoon natural vanilla extract
150 g (5$\frac{1}{2}$ oz) unsalted butter, melted and cooled
240 g (8$\frac{3}{4}$ oz/1 cup) mashed ripe banana

MAKES 12

Preheat the oven to 200°C (400°F/Gas 6). Lightly grease a 12-hole standard muffin tin, or line the muffin tin with paper cases. Sift the flour into a bowl. Add the sugar and mixed spice to the bowl and stir through the flour. Make a well in the centre.

Mix together the milk, egg and vanilla. Pour the liquid into the well in the flour and add the cooled butter and banana. Fold the mixture gently with a metal spoon until just combined. Do not overmix — the batter will still be slightly lumpy. Divide the mixture evenly among the holes — fill each hole to about three-quarters full.

Bake the muffins for 20-25 minutes, or until they are golden and a skewer inserted into the centre of a muffin comes out clean. Leave the muffins in the tin for a couple of minutes to cool. Gently loosen each muffin with a flat-bladed knife before turning out onto a wire rack. Serve warm or at room temperature.

PREPARATION TIME: 20 MINUTES   COOKING TIME: 25 MINUTES

Chocolate-chip muffins

BUTTERFLY CAKES

120 g (4¼ oz) unsalted butter, softened

145 g (5½ oz/⅔ cup) caster (superfine) sugar

185 g (6½ oz/1½ cups) self-raising flour

125 ml (4 fl oz/½ cup) milk

2 teaspoons natural vanilla extract

2 eggs

125 ml (4 fl oz/½ cup) pouring (whipping) cream

105 g (3¾ oz/⅓ cup) strawberry jam

icing (confectioners') sugar, to dust

MAKES 12

Preheat the oven to 180°C (350°F/Gas 4). Line a 12-hole shallow patty pan or mini muffin tin with paper cases.

Put the butter, sugar, flour, milk, vanilla and eggs in a bowl and beat, using electric beaters on low speed for 2 minutes, or until well mixed. Increase the speed and beat for 2 minutes, or until smooth and pale.

Divide the mixture evenly among the cases and bake for 20 minutes, or until cooked and golden. Transfer to a wire rack to cool completely.

Whip the cream to soft peaks. Using a small sharp knife, cut shallow rounds from the top of each cake. Cut these in half. Spoon ½ tablespoon of the cream into the cavity in each cake, then top with 1 teaspoon of the jam. Position two halves of the cake tops in the jam in each cake to resemble butterfly wings. Dust the cakes with icing sugar before serving.

PREPARATION TIME: 20 MINUTES +   COOKING TIME: 20 MINUTES

NOTE: To make iced cup cakes, don't cut off the tops. Mix 60 g (2¼ oz/½ cup) sifted icing (confectioners') sugar, 1 teaspoon softened unsalted butter, ½ teaspoon natural vanilla extract and up to 3 teaspoons hot water to form a smooth paste, then spread the icing (frosting) on the cooled cakes.

ORANGE CUP CAKES

120 g (4¼ oz) unsalted butter, softened
145 g (5½ oz/⅔ cup) caster (superfine) sugar
185 g (6½ oz/1½ cups) self-raising flour
125 ml (4 fl oz/½ cup) orange juice
2 teaspoons natural vanilla extract
2 eggs
3 tablespoons grated orange zest
shredded orange zest, to decorate (optional)

ICING
60 g (2¼ oz) unsalted butter, softened
90 g (3¼ oz/¾ cup) icing (confectioners') sugar
1 tablespoon orange juice

MAKES 12

Preheat the oven to 180°C (350°F/Gas 4). Line a deep 12-hole patty pan or mini muffin tin with paper cases. Place the butter, sugar, flour, orange juice, vanilla and eggs in a bowl and beat using electric beaters on low speed for 2 minutes, or until well mixed. Increase the speed and beat for 2 minutes, or until smooth and pale. Stir in the orange zest. Divide among the cases and bake for 20 minutes, or until golden. Transfer to a wire rack to cool completely.

To make the icing (frosting), beat the butter in a bowl using electric beaters until pale. Beat in half the icing sugar, all the orange juice, then the remaining icing sugar. Spread over the cakes, then decorate if desired.

PREPARATION TIME: 15 MINUTES +   COOKING TIME: 20 MINUTES

PEANUT CHOC-CHIP MUFFINS

250 g (9 oz/2 cups) self-raising flour
75 g (2¾ oz/⅓ cup) raw sugar
265 g (9½ oz/1½ cups) dark chocolate chips
1 egg
250 g (9 oz/1 cup) crunchy peanut butter
2 tablespoons strawberry jam
60 g (2¼ oz) unsalted butter, melted
250 ml (9 fl oz/1 cup) milk
icing (confectioners') sugar, to dust

MAKES 12

Preheat oven to 180°C (350°F/Gas 4). Lightly grease a 12-hole standard muffin tin, or line the muffin tin with paper cases.

Sift the flour into a large bowl. Add the sugar and chocolate chips and make a well in the centre. Combine the egg, peanut butter, jam, butter and milk and add to the flour. Stir until just combined. Do not overmix — the batter will still be slightly lumpy.

Divide the mixture evenly among the holes — fill each hole to about three-quarters full. Bake for 20–25 minutes, or until golden and a skewer inserted into the centre of a muffin comes out clean. Leave the muffins in the tin for a couple of minutes to cool. Gently loosen each muffin with a flat-bladed knife, before turning out onto a wire rack. Dust with icing sugar. Serve warm or at room temperature.

PREPARATION TIME: 15 MINUTES   COOKING TIME: 25 MINUTES

DOUBLE CHOCOLATE COOKIES

185 g (6¹/₂ oz/1¹/₂ cups) plain (all-purpose) flour
90 g (3¹/₄ oz/³/₄ cup) unsweetened cocoa powder
280 g (10 oz/1¹/₂ cups) soft brown sugar
180 g (6¹/₂ oz) unsalted butter, cubed
150 g (5¹/₂ oz) dark chocolate, chopped
3 eggs, lightly beaten
265 g (9¹/₂ oz/1¹/₂ cups) chocolate chips

MAKES 40

Preheat the oven to 180°C (350°F/Gas 4). Line two baking trays with baking paper.

Sift the flour and cocoa powder into a large bowl, add the soft brown sugar and make a well in the centre.

Combine the butter and dark chocolate in a small heatproof bowl. Bring a saucepan of water to the boil, then remove the pan from the heat. Sit the heatproof bowl over the pan, making sure the base of the bowl does not touch the water. Stir occasionally until the chocolate and butter have melted and are smooth. Mix well.

Add the butter and chocolate mixture and the egg to the dry ingredients. Stir with a wooden spoon until well combined, but do not overbeat. Stir in the chocolate chips. Drop tablespoons of the mixture onto the trays, allowing room for spreading. Bake for 7–10 minutes, or until firm to the touch. Cool on the trays for 5 minutes before transferring to a wire rack to cool completely. When the cookies are completely cold, store in an airtight container.

PREPARATION TIME: 20 MINUTES   COOKING TIME: 10 MINUTES

NOTE: When dropping the dough onto the tray, it is easier and less messy to use two tablespoons, one to measure accurately and the other to push the dough off the spoon onto the tray.

MUESLI SLICE

250 g (9 oz) unsalted butter, cubed
230 g (8$\frac{1}{2}$ oz/1 cup) caster (superfine) sugar
2 tablespoons honey
250 g (9 oz/2$\frac{1}{2}$ cups) rolled (porridge) oats
65 g (2$\frac{1}{2}$ oz/$\frac{3}{4}$ cup) desiccated coconut
30 g (1 oz/1 cup) cornflakes, lightly crushed
45 g (1$\frac{3}{4}$ oz/$\frac{1}{2}$ cup) flaked almonds
1 teaspoon ground mixed (pumpkin pie) spice
45 g (1$\frac{3}{4}$ oz) finely chopped dried apricots
185 g (6$\frac{1}{2}$ oz/1 cup) dried mixed fruit

MAKES 18

Preheat the oven to 160°C (315°F/Gas 2–3). Lightly grease a shallow tin measuring 20 x 30 cm (8 x 12 inches) and line with baking paper, leaving the paper hanging over on the two long sides.

Put the butter, sugar and honey in a small saucepan and stir over low heat for 5 minutes, or until the butter has melted and the sugar has dissolved.

Mix the remaining ingredients together in a bowl and make a well in the centre. Pour in the butter mixture and stir well, then press into the tin. Bake for 45 minutes, or until golden. Cool completely in the tin, then refrigerate for 2 hours, to firm.

Lift the slice from the tin, using the paper as handles, before cutting into pieces. This slice will keep for up to 3 days stored in an airtight container.

PREPARATION TIME: 20 MINUTES +   COOKING TIME: 50 MINUTES

MUESLI CHEWS

4 wheat breakfast biscuits, crushed
100 g (3$\frac{1}{2}$ oz/1 cup) rolled (porridge) oats
45 g (1$\frac{3}{4}$ oz/$\frac{1}{2}$ cup) desiccated coconut
95 g (3$\frac{1}{2}$ oz/$\frac{1}{2}$ cup) soft brown sugar
125 g (4$\frac{1}{2}$ oz) unsalted butter, melted
1 tablespoon honey

MAKES 20

Preheat the oven to 180°C (350°F/Gas 4). Line an 18 x 28 cm (7 x 11$\frac{1}{4}$ inch) Swiss roll tin (jelly roll tin) with baking paper, leaving the paper hanging over the two long sides.

In a large bowl, combine the biscuits, oats, coconut and sugar. Stir in the butter and honey.

Press firmly into the tin. Bake for 15 minutes, or until golden. Cool in the tin, then lift out and cut into squares with a sharp knife.

PREPARATION TIME: 15 MINUTES   COOKING TIME: 15 MINUTES

MARBLED BISCUITS

180 g (6½ oz) unsalted butter, softened

230 g (8½ oz/1 cup) caster (superfine) sugar

1 teaspoon natural vanilla extract

1 egg

a few drops red food colouring

50 g (1¾ oz) dark chocolate, melted

1 tablespoon unsweetened cocoa powder

2 teaspoons milk

270 g (9½ oz) plain (all-purpose) flour

¾ teaspoon baking powder

MAKES ABOUT 60

Cream the butter and sugar in a small bowl using electric beaters until light and creamy. Add the vanilla and egg and beat until well combined. Divide the creamed butter and egg mixture into three bowls.

Add the food colouring to one and the melted chocolate, cocoa powder and milk to another. Leave one plain. Add one-third of the sifted flour and ¼ teaspoon baking powder to each bowl.

Using a flat-bladed knife, mix each to a soft dough, then divide in half and roll into thin logs. Twist the three colours together to create a marbled effect, then shape the combined dough into two logs. Refrigerate for 30 minutes, or until firm.

Preheat the oven to 180°C (350°F/Gas 4). Line two baking trays with baking paper.

Cut the logs into slices about 1 cm (½ inch) thick. Place on the prepared trays, leaving 3 cm (1¼ inches) between each slice. Bake for 10–15 minutes, or until golden. Cool on the trays for 3 minutes before transferring to a wire rack to cool completely. When cold, store in an airtight container.

PREPARATION TIME: 30 MINUTES +   COOKING TIME: 15 MINUTES

CORNFLAKE COOKIES

125 g (4½ oz) unsalted butter, softened
165 g (5¾ oz/¾ cup) sugar
2 eggs, lightly beaten
1 teaspoon natural vanilla extract
2 tablespoons currants
135 g (4¾ oz/1½ cups) desiccated coconut
½ teaspoon bicarbonate of soda (baking soda)
½ teaspoon baking powder
250 g (9 oz/2 cups) plain (all-purpose) flour
90 g (3¼ oz/3 cups) cornflakes, lightly crushed

MAKES 36

Preheat the oven to 180°C (350°F/Gas 4). Line two baking trays with baking paper. Cream the butter and sugar in a small bowl using electric beaters until light and fluffy. Gradually add the egg, beating thoroughly after each addition. Add the vanilla and beat until combined.

Transfer the mixture to a large bowl and stir in the currants and coconut. Fold in the sifted bicarbonate of soda, baking powder and flour with a metal spoon and stir until the mixture is almost smooth. Put the cornflakes in a shallow dish, then drop level tablespoons of mixture onto the cornflakes and roll into balls. Arrange on the trays, allowing room for spreading.

Bake for 15–20 minutes, or until crisp and golden. Cool slightly on the tray before transferring to a wire rack to cool. When completely cold, store in an airtight container.

PREPARATION TIME: 15 MINUTES   COOKING TIME: 20 MINUTES

NUTTY BISCUITS

125 g (4½ oz) unsalted butter, softened
115 g (4 oz/½ cup) caster (superfine) sugar
60 ml (2 fl oz/¼ cup) milk
¼ teaspoon natural vanilla extract
60 g (2¼ oz/½ cup) finely chopped walnuts or pecans
185 g (6½ oz/1½ cups) self-raising flour
60 g (2¼ oz/½ cup) custard powder or instant vanilla pudding mix
nuts, to decorate

MAKES 30

Line two baking trays with baking paper or lightly grease with some melted butter. Preheat the oven to 210°C (415°F/Gas 6–7) and check the racks are near the centre. Cut the butter into cubes and cream with the caster sugar in a small bowl using electric beaters, or by hand, until light and creamy. Scrape down the side of the bowl occasionally with a spatula. The mixture should look pale and be quite smooth. The sugar should be almost dissolved. Add the milk and vanilla and beat until combined. Add the nuts and mix well. Add the self-raising flour and custard powder and use a flat-bladed knife to bring to a soft dough.

Rotate the bowl as you work and use a cutting action to incorporate the dry ingredients. Don't overwork the dough or you will end up with tough biscuits (cookies). Roll level teaspoons into balls and place on the trays, leaving 5 cm (2 inches) between each biscuit. Flatten the balls lightly with your fingertips, then press a nut onto each biscuit. The biscuits should be about 5 cm (2 inches) in diameter. Bake for 15–18 minutes, or until lightly golden. Cool on the trays for 3 minutes before transferring to a wire rack to cool completely.

PREPARATION TIME: 15 MINUTES   COOKING TIME: 20 MINUTES

Cornflake cookies

CHOCOLATE CAKE

125 g (4¹/₂ oz) unsalted butter, softened
115 g (4 oz/¹/₂ cup) caster (superfine) sugar
40 g (1¹/₂ oz/¹/₃ cup) icing (confectioners')
sugar, sifted
2 eggs, lightly beaten
1 teaspoon natural vanilla extract
80 g (2³/₄ oz/¹/₄ cup) blackberry jam
155 g (5¹/₂ oz/1¹/₄ cups) self-raising flour
60 g (2¹/₄ oz/¹/₂ cup) unsweetened cocoa
powder
1 teaspoon bicarbonate of soda
(baking soda)
250 ml (9 fl oz/1 cup) milk

CHOCOLATE BUTTERCREAM
50 g (1³/₄ oz) dark chocolate, finely
chopped
25 g (1 oz) unsalted butter
3 teaspoons pouring (whipping) cream
30 g (1 oz/¹/₄ cup) icing (confectioners')
sugar, sifted

SERVES 8–10

Preheat the oven to 180°C (350°F/Gas 4). Lightly grease a 20 cm (8 inch) square cake tin and line with baking paper.

Cream the butter and sugars in a small bowl using electric beaters until light and fluffy. Add the eggs gradually, beating thoroughly after each addition. Beat in the vanilla and jam. Transfer to a large bowl. Using a metal spoon, gently fold in the combined sifted flour, cocoa powder and bicarbonate of soda alternately with the milk. Stir until the mixture is just combined and almost smooth.

Pour into the tin and smooth the surface. Bake for 45 minutes, or until a skewer inserted into the centre of the cake comes out clean. Leave in the tin for 15 minutes before turning out onto a wire rack to cool completely.

To make the buttercream, stir the ingredients in a small saucepan over low heat until smooth and glossy. Spread over the top of the cake with a flat-bladed knife.

PREPARATION TIME: 25 MINUTES +   COOKING TIME: 50 MINUTES

CHOCOLATE MALLOW FUDGE

70 g (2½ oz) unsalted butter, chopped
150 g (5½ oz) dark chocolate, chopped
250 g (9 oz) white marshmallows
1 teaspoon natural vanilla extract
50 g (1¾ oz) milk chocolate

MAKES ABOUT 40

Line the base and two long sides of an 8 x 26 cm (3¼ x 10½ inch) loaf (bar) tin with foil.

Put the butter, chocolate and marshmallows in a saucepan. Stir constantly over low heat until the chocolate and marshmallows have melted. Remove the pan from the heat and stir in the vanilla.

Pour the mixture into the tin and refrigerate for several hours, or overnight, until firm.

Remove the fudge from the tin and remove the foil. Cut into 2 cm (¾ inch) slices, then cut each slice into three pieces. Melt the milk chocolate and drizzle over the fudge, then set aside until set.

PREPARATION TIME: 20 MINUTES +   COOKING TIME: 10 MINUTES

CHOCOLATE FINGERS

2 egg whites
115 g (4 oz/½ cup) caster (superfine) sugar
1 tablespoon sifted unsweetened cocoa powder
melted chocolate, to serve (optional)
unsweetened cocoa powder and icing (confectioners') sugar, to serve (optional)

MAKES 40

Preheat the oven to 150°C (300°F/Gas 2) and line two baking trays with baking paper.

Beat the egg whites into stiff peaks in a small dry bowl using electric beaters. Add the caster sugar, 1 tablespoon at a time, beating well after each addition. Beat until the mixture is thick and glossy and the sugar has dissolved (this will take up to 10 minutes), then beat in the cocoa powder

Spoon the mixture into a piping (icing) bag fitted with a plain round nozzle and pipe fine 8 cm (3¼ inch) lengths onto lined trays, allowing room for spreading.

Bake for 20-25 minutes, or until pale and dry. Serve as they are, drizzled with melted chocolate or lightly dusted with dark cocoa powder combined with a little icing sugar.

PREPARATION TIME: 20 MINUTES   COOKING TIME: 25 MINUTES

Chocolate mallow fudge

CHERRY CAKE

210 g (7½ oz/1 cup) glacé cherries
85 g (3 oz/⅔ cup) plain (all-purpose) flour
90 g (3¼ oz) unsalted butter, softened
145 g (5½ oz/⅔ cup) caster (superfine) sugar
2 eggs, lightly beaten
1 teaspoon natural vanilla extract
125 g (4½ oz/1 cup) self-raising flour
80 ml (2½ fl oz/⅓ cup) milk

ICING
125 g (4½ oz/1 cup) icing (confectioners') sugar
20 g (¾ oz) unsalted butter
pink food colouring

SERVES 8–10

Preheat the oven to 180°C (350°F/Gas 4). Grease a 20 cm (8 inch) kugelhopf tin. Dust with flour, then shake off any excess. Rinse and dry the glacé cherries and cut each in half. Toss them in a little of the flour.

Cream the butter and sugar in a small bowl using electric beaters until light and fluffy. Add the egg gradually, beating thoroughly after each addition. Beat in the vanilla. Transfer to a large bowl. Using a large metal spoon, fold in the sifted flours alternately with the milk. Stir in the cherries. Spoon into the tin and smooth the surface. Bake for 35 minutes, or until a skewer inserted into the centre of the cake comes out clean. Leave in the tin for 10 minutes before turning out onto a wire rack to cool completely.

To make the icing (frosting), combine the sifted icing sugar, butter and 1–2 tablespoons water in a small heatproof bowl. Stand the bowl over a saucepan of simmering water, making sure that the base of the bowl does not touch the water. Stir the mixture until the butter has melted and the icing is glossy and smooth. Stir in a couple of drops of food colouring. Drizzle over the cake, allowing it to run down the sides.

PREPARATION TIME: 30 MINUTES +   COOKING TIME: 40 MINUTES

UPSIDE-DOWN BANANA CAKE

50 g (1³/₄ oz) unsalted butter, melted

60 g (2¹/₄ oz/¹/₃ cup) soft brown sugar

6 very ripe large bananas, halved lengthways

125 g (4¹/₂ oz) unsalted butter, extra, softened

230 g (8¹/₂ oz/1¹/₄ cups) soft brown sugar, extra

2 eggs, lightly beaten

185 g (6¹/₂ oz/1¹/₂ cups) self-raising flour

1 teaspoon baking powder

2 large bananas, extra, mashed

SERVES 8

Preheat the oven to 180°C (350°F/Gas 4). Grease and line a 20 cm (8 inch) square cake tin, pour the melted butter over the base of the tin and sprinkle with the sugar. Arrange the bananas, cut side down, over the brown sugar. Cream the butter and extra brown sugar using electric beaters until light and fluffy. Add the eggs gradually, beating well after each addition.

Sift the flour and baking powder into a bowl, then fold into the cake mixture with the mashed banana. Carefully spread into the tin. Bake for 45 minutes, or until a skewer inserted into the centre of the cake comes out clean. Turn out onto a wire rack while still warm.

PREPARATION TIME: 20 MINUTES   COOKING TIME: 45 MINUTES

SULTANA CAKE

250 g (9 oz) unsalted butter, softened

230 g (8¹/₂ oz/1 cup) caster (superfine) sugar

3 eggs, lightly beaten

2 teaspoons grated lemon zest

1 teaspoon natural vanilla extract

250 g (9 oz/2 cups) sultanas (golden raisins)

375 g (13 oz/3 cups) plain (all-purpose) flour

1¹/₂ teaspoons baking powder

170 ml (5¹/₂ fl oz/²/₃ cup) buttermilk

SERVES 8–10

Preheat the oven to 160°C (315°F/Gas 2–3). Lightly grease and line a 20 cm (8 inch) square cake tin.

Cream the butter and sugar in a small bowl using electric beaters until light and fluffy. Gradually add the egg, beating thoroughly after each addition. Beat in the lemon zest and vanilla. Transfer to a large bowl. Using a metal spoon, fold in the sultanas and sifted flour and baking powder, alternately with the buttermilk. Spoon into the tin and smooth the surface. Bake for 1¹/₄–1¹/₂ hours, or until a skewer inserted into the centre of the cake comes out clean. Cool in the tin for 20 minutes before turning out onto a wire rack.

PREPARATION TIME: 20 MINUTES   COOKING TIME: 1 HOUR 30 MINUTES

Upside-down banana cake

INDEX

INDEX

A

afghans 173

almonds
  almond torte 205
  almond-crusted cheese bites 225
  amandine 53
  orange and almond cake 89
  plum and almond slice 25
  praline triangles 58

amandine 53

anchovy and tomato crostini 97

angel food cake 197

aniseed biscuits 33

Anzac biscuits 157

apples
  apple and spice teacake 181
  apple cinnamon muffins 45
  apple mousseline mayonnaise 126
  beignets de fruits 61
  curried apple and onion mini quiche 109

artichokes, Florentine scones with mortadella and artichoke 129

B

baguette with egg, dill pesto and prosciutto 121

bakewell tart 201

bananas
  banana cake 73
  banana muffins 229
  upside-down banana cake 249

beef, roast beef, pâté and rocket fingers 133

beignets de fruits 61

biscuits
  afghans 173
  aniseed biscuits 33
  Anzac biscuits 157
  brandy snaps 158
  brown sugar shortbread 145
  cheese biscuits 213
  chocolate peppermint creams 54
  chocolate wheat biscuits 37
  citrus biscuits 42
  coffee kisses 149
  cornflake cookies 241
  double chocolate cookies 234
  digestive biscuits 141
  Fig Newtons 169
  florentines 161
  ginger shortbread 45
  gingernuts 157
  graham crackers 101
  Greek shortbread 21
  honey biscuits 65
  lebkuchen 150
  lemon and lime biscuits 29
  macadamia biscuits 25
  maple and pecan biscuits 30
  marbled biscuits 238
  melting moments 149
  monte creams 37
  nutty biscuits 241
  peanut biscuits 41
  spicy fruit biscuits 21
  Viennese fingers 34
  see also shortbread

Black Forest gâteau 206

blueberry cheesecake 74

blueberry muffins 17

brandy snaps 158

breads
  finger buns 226
  light fruit bread 170
  Sally Lunn bread 166
  brown sugar shortbread 145

brownies
  cappuccino 65
  chocolate 29
  jaffa triple-chocolate 85

butter frosting 73

butterfly cakes 230

C

cakes
  almond torte 205
  angel food cake 197
  banana cake 73
  Black Forest gâteau 206
  boiled fruit cake 197
  butterfly cakes 230
  carrot cake 189
  cherry cake 246
  chocolate cake 242
  chocolate éclairs 198
  chocolate mud cake 89
  coconut cake 92
  cream buns 220
  Eccles cakes 169
  flourless chocolate cake 69
  ginger cake 90
  golden fruit cake 205
  hazelnut and chocolate friands 10
  hummingbird cake 202
  lamingtons 162
  lemon cake with crunchy topping 77
  lemon coconut cake 73
  lumberjack cake 66
  Madeira cake 189
  madeleines 161
  meringue and berry cake 82
  orange and almond cake 89
  orange cake 185
  orange cup cakes 233
  orange and lemon syrup cake 86
  orange poppy seed cake 186
  parkin 165
  pound cake 185
  Sacher torte 85
  seed cake 193
  sultana cake 249
  see also brownies; sponge; Swiss roll; upside-down cake

cappuccino brownies 65

capsicum
    capsicum rolls 105
    roast capsicum rice tarts 110
caramel
    chocolate cups with caramel 49
    hard caramels 41
carrot cake 189
caviar eggs 125
cheese
    almond-crusted cheese bites 225
    cheese biscuits 213
    cheese scones 97
    cheese twists 213
    pan-fried cheese sandwiches 105
    soft cheese pâté 101
    see also cheesecake
cheesecake
    blueberry 74
    chocolate collar 81
    mini cheesecakes 81
    New York cheesecake 190
Chelsea buns 174
cherries
    cherry cake 246
    teardrop chocolate cherry
        mousse cups 62
chicken
    chicken and corn bites 225
    chicken liver pâté with pistachios
        and prosciutto 117
    chicken rolls 106
    chicken sausage rolls 98
    chicken strips with sweet and
        sour sauce 210
    chicken tamales 94
    crispy chicken and fish wraps
        with sweet and sour sauce 218
    sesame chicken sticks 222
chips, golden potato 221
chocolate
    chocolate-chip muffins 229
    chocolate brownies 29
    chocolate buttercream 242

chocolate cake 242
chocolate clusters 49
chocolate collar cheesecake 81
chocolate cups with caramel 49
chocolate éclairs 198
chocolate fingers 245
chocolate mallow fudge 245
chocolate meringue kisses 53
chocolate mousse 62
chocolate mud cake 89
chocolate peppermint creams
   54
chocolate peppermint slice 38
chocolate Swiss roll 77
chocolate tarts 50
chocolate wheat biscuits 37
double chocolate cookies 234
double chocolate muffins 61
flourless chocolate cake 69
hazelnut and chocolate friands 10
jaffa triple-choc brownies 85
mini cheesecakes 81
peanut choc-chip muffins 233
praline triangles 58
rich chocolate truffles 57
teardrop chocolate cherry
    mousse cups 62
white cake truffles 57
cinnamon teacake 181
citrus biscuits 42
coconut
    coconut icing 73
    coconut jam slice 145
    lemon coconut cake 73
muesli chews 237
muesli slice 237
coffee
    coffee buttercream 149
    coffee cream 22
    coffee kisses 149
    pecan coffee slice 22
Continental slice 26
cookies see biscuits

corn
    chicken and corn bites 225
    ham and corn relish fingers 133
    corn dogs, mini 217
    cornflake cookies 241
crab and spring onion mini quiches
   117
cream buns 194
crostini, anchovy and tomato 97
crunchy peanut meringue slice 33
curry
    curried apple and onion mini
        quiche 109
    individual pumpkin and curry
        quiches 109
    spicy vegetable muffins 113
custard rolls 153

D
date and walnut rolls 177
digestive biscuits 141
dill pesto 121
doughnuts, Israeli 18
duck, warm duck and coriander
    tartlets 122

E
Eccles cakes 169
éclairs, chocolate 198
eggs
    baguette with egg, dill pesto and
        prosciutto 121
    caviar eggs 125
English muffins 138

F
Fig Newtons 169
finger buns 226
Florentine scones with mortadella
    and artichoke 129
florentines 161
flourless chocolate cake 69
frankfurts, mini corn dogs 217

fruit
    beignets de fruits 61
    boiled fruit cake 197
    fruit mince slice 165
    golden fruit cake 205
    hummingbird cake 202
    light fruit bread 170
    spicy fruit biscuits 21

G
garlic toast with salmon mayonnaise 125
Genoise sponge 201
ginger
    ginger cake 90
    ginger shortbread 45
    gingernuts 157
golden fruit cake 205
golden potato chips 221
graham crackers 101
Greek shortbread 21

H
ham and corn relish fingers 133
hard caramels 41
hazelnuts
    amandine 53
    hazelnut and chocolate friands 10
honey biscuits 65
honey cream roll 70
hummingbird cake 202

I
Israeli doughnuts 18

J
jaffa triple-choc brownies 85

L
lamb
    lamb on polenta 129
    spicy lamb sausage rolls 113
lamingtons 162

lebkuchen 150
lemon
    citrus biscuits 42
    lemon and ginger icing 90
    lemon and lime biscuits 29
    lemon cake with crunchy topping 77
    lemon coconut cake 73
    lemon icing 189
    orange and lemon syrup cake 86
    lumberjack cake 66

M
macadamia biscuits 25
Madeira cake 189
madeleines 161
maple and pecan biscuits 30
marbled biscuits 238
meatballs 217
melting moments 149
meringue
    chocolate meringue kisses 53
    crunchy peanut meringue slice 33
    meringue and berry cake 82
monte creams 37
mud cake, chocolate 89
muesli chews 237
muesli slice 237
muffins
    apple cinnamon muffins 45
    banana muffins 229
    blueberry muffins 17
    choc chip muffins 229
    double chocolate muffins 61
    English muffins 138
    orange poppy seed muffins 14
    peanut choc-chip muffins 233
    pecan muffins 17
    spicy vegetable muffins 113
    strawberry and passionfruit muffins 46

N
neenish tarts 154
New York cheesecake 190
nut meringue 33
nutty biscuits 241

O
onions
    crab and spring onion mini quiches 117
    curried apple and onion mini quiche 109
oranges
    orange and almond cake 89
    orange buttercream 185
    orange cake 185
    orange cup cakes 233
    orange and lemon syrup cake 86
    orange poppy seed cake 186
    orange poppy seed muffins 14

P
parkin 165
pâté
    chicken liver pâté with pistachios and prosciutto 117
    smoked salmon pâté with chive pikelets 114
    soft cheese pâté 101
peanuts
    crunchy peanut meringue slice 33
    peanut biscuits 41
    peanut choc-chip muffins 233
pecans
    maple and pecan biscuits 30
    pecan coffee slice 22
    ecan muffins 17
peppermint
    chocolate peppermint creams 54
    chocolate peppermint slice 38
pineapple upside-down cake 193
plum and almond slice 25

poppy seeds
    orange poppy seed cake 186
    orange poppy seed muffins 14
potatoes
    golden potato chips 221
    potato noodle nibbles 221
pound cake 185
praline triangles 58
prawns, potted 121
princess fingers 173
pumpkin
    individual pumpkin and curry
        quiches 109
    pumpkin and sage scones 141
    pumpkin scones 13

Q
quiches
    individual pumpkin and curry 109
    mini crab and spring onion 117
    mini curried apple and onion 109
    mini smoked salmon 134
    quiche Lorraine 142

R
rice, roast capsicum rice tarts 110
rolls, savoury
    capsicum rolls 105
    chicken rolls 106
    chicken sausage rolls 98
    chicken tamales 94
    sausage rolls 214
    smoked salmon rolls 18
    spicy lamb sausage rolls 102
rolls, sweet
    custard rolls 153
    date and walnut rolls 177
    honey cream roll 70
    see also Swiss roll

S
Sacher torte 85
Sally Lunn bread 166

salmon
    garlic toast with salmon
        mayonnaise 125
    smoked salmon mini quiches
        134
    smoked salmon pâté with chive
        pikelets 114
    smoked salmon rolls 102
sandwiches
    ham and corn relish fingers 133
    pan-fried cheese sandwiches 105
    roast beef, pâté and rocket
        fingers 133
sausage rolls 214
scones 142
    cheese scones 97
    Florentine scones with
        mortadella and artichoke 129
    pumpkin and sage scones 141
    pumpkin scones 13
    sultana scones 13
seafood
    crab and spring onion mini
        quiches 117
    crispy chicken and fish wraps
        with sweet and sour sauce 218
    garlic toast with salmon
        mayonnaise 125
    potted prawns 121
    seafood parcels 118
    smoked salmon mini quiches
        134
    smoked salmon pâté with chive
        pikelets 114
    smoked salmon rolls 102
    tuna tartlets with apple
        mousseline mayonnaise 126
seed cake 193
sesame chicken sticks 222
shortbread
    brown sugar 145
    ginger 45
    Greek 21

slices
    chocolate peppermint slice 38
    coconut jam slice 145
    Continental slice 26
    crunchy peanut meringue slice
        33
    fruit mince slice 165
    muesli slice 237
    pecan coffee slice 22
    plum and almond slice 25
    princess fingers 173
    vanilla slice 146
spicy fruit biscuits 21
spicy lamb sausage rolls 113
spicy vegetable muffins 113
sponge
    classic sponge 182
    Genoise sponge 201
    strawberries and cream sponge
        with spun toffee 78
strawberries
    strawberries and cream sponge
        with spun toffee 78
    strawberry and passionfruit
        muffins 46
    strawberry Swiss roll 69
sultana cake 249
sultana scones 13
Swedish tea ring 178
sweet and sour sauces 210, 218, 222
sweets
    chocolate mallow fudge 245
    hard caramels 41
Swiss roll 177
    chocolate 77
    strawberry 69

T
tarts
    bakewell tart 201
    chocolate tart 50
    neenish tarts 154
    roast capsicum rice tarts 110

tarts continued
    tuna tartlets with apple
        mousseline mayonnaise 126
    warm duck and coriander tartlets
        122
teacakes
    apple and spice 181
    cinnamon 181
    Swedish tea ring 178
teardrop chocolate cherry mousse
        cups 62
truffles
    rich chocolate 57
    white cake 57
tuna tartlets with apple mousseline
      mayonnaise 126

U
upside-down cake
    banana 249
    pineapple 193

V
vanilla slice 146
vegetable muffins, spicy 113
Viennese fingers 34

W
white cake truffles 57